SHEFFIELD FOOTBALL CLUB
150 YEARS OF FOOTBALL

1857

SHEFFIELD F.C.

THE WORLD'S FIRST FOOTBALL CLUB

Written by Steven Hutton, Graham Curry and Peter Goodman

at heart publications

Sheffield FC would like to thank the following companies for their contribution to the publication of this book:

Sheffield United Football Club
Bright Finance Limited
Thornbridge Brewery
A4e
David Cartwright
Forde Recruitment
Price Waterhouse Coopers
Stauff UK Limited
Proco Print
Webbworlds
Charles James and Co.
G & J Hall Limited
Fyfe Financial
GVT
S & L Electrical
TDC
Iris Associates
Pete Bowden Sports Ground Maintenance
Onside Law
Birch International Carpets
Rocket Science
Royal Bank of Scotland Group
Rillatech Ltd
Ashton Morton Slack
Northern Counties Housing Association
The Workshop
Rider Levet Bucknall

First Published in 2007 by:
At Heart Ltd, 32 Stamford Street, Altrincham,
Cheshire, WA14 1EY.
in conjunction with
Sheffield FC

Printed by Bell & Bain, Scotland.

ISBN: 978 1 84547 174 3

Contents

Foreword / 4

Introduction / 5

Hall of Fame / 6

Football Seeds Sown in Greenhouse / 10

In the Beginning / 11

Creswick and Prest / 21

At Last… Teams to Play! / 26

London and the Football Association / 31

The FA Cup / 35

Sheffield's Football Influence / 38

Amateur Cup Triumph / 42

Fight Against Professionalism / 47

The Grounds / 50

Centenary Celebrations / 57

Club on Tour / 73

FA Vase Cup / 92

Unusual Opponents / 97

Annual Dinners / 101

Tough Times for Club / 105

FIFA Order of Merit / 107

Bright Future / 115

Football Reaches 150th Milestone / 128

150 Years of Memories / 134

Happy Birthday Sheffield / 142

Acknowledgements / 143

Bibliography / 144

Foreword

I WOULD firstly like to offer my congratulations to Sheffield FC for reaching this unique milestone. This is a remarkable achievement and one which the club and the rest of the football world should be proud of.

Sheffield FC is where it all began and their position is unique within the game. When the club was launched 150 years ago, I'm sure no-one would have thought how successful and global football would become.

The sport has come a long way during that period, with 270million people from all countries around the world now playing and billions watching the beautiful game.

FIFA was pleased to present Sheffield FC with the Order of Merit in Paris in 2004, a great achievement by an amateur outfit considering the only other club to receive the prestigious accolade is Real Madrid.

Since the presentation, I have taken great interest in their fortunes. Chairman Richard Tims has spoken with me and my colleagues on a number of occasions about how Sheffield FC are progressing both on and off the field. We know they are using their special place in football for the benefit of the community on a local, national and international level, which is great to hear.

Their Boots for Africa campaign is a fantastic initiative and one we applaud at FIFA as it continues our aims of ensuring football is made available to all and helping to build a better future.

Richard asked if I would become a member of the oldest football club in the world and I was delighted to join. I am happy to see some of my colleagues at FIFA have also become members. Supporting the oldest club is a way of supporting the whole of football no matter who your allegiances are with.

I would again like to offer my best wishes to Sheffield FC for reaching 150 years and we hope they will continue to play an important role in football for another 150 years.

Best regards
Sepp Blatter
FIFA President

Introduction

IT IS A momentous achievement by Sheffield FC and in fact football as a whole that we have reached 150 years. Sheffield FC is where club football began, a fact recognised by the English Football Association and the Fédération Internationale de Football Association (FIFA).

No other club in the world enjoys such an extensive history as Sheffield FC and I am pleased to mark the anniversary with this unique book, highlighting all the key moments and achievements that have taken place during this time.

The club's amateur status has continued from the first meeting on 24 October 1857 to the current day and our commitment of 'Playing for the Love of the Game' is as strong in 2007 as it was in the days of founders Nathaniel Creswick and William Prest.

However, Sheffield FC has changed dramatically from those early days and great strides have been made in the last few years to put the club and city on the map, locally, nationally and internationally.

We now own our stadium for the first time in 150 years, have three senior sides and also provide football opportunities to 13 junior teams, two girls' teams, a women's side and three disability teams.

The club embodies everything that is good about grassroots football and the positive role it can play in the community.

We provide an Inclusion and Diversity Scheme in conjunction with the Football Foundation to help increase participation in sport and physical activity for people with disability. While our Boots for Africa campaign will make football more accessible to thousands of young people in South Africa.

More than 30 businesses provide their much-needed support and backing with sponsorship and the club has formed important links with international football clubs such as Real Madrid.

Sheffield FC has been working closely with the Sheffield Chamber of Commerce, who also celebrate their 150th anniversary in 2007, bringing business and football together in a special partnership, which we hope will last for many years to come.

The club has a unique link with the Chamber as the first Sheffield Chamber of Commerce President Edward Vickers was the father of Thomas Edward Vickers, an original committee member of Sheffield FC when it formed in 1857.

I would like to take this opportunity to thank everyone who has played a role at Sheffield FC over the years and helped to make the club what it is today. The support of so many people behind the scenes, often on a voluntary basis, is and has been greatly appreciated.

May I also thank our club historian Graham Curry for his hard work and committed devotion to finding the facts about Sheffield FC. The day we fortuitously met at a Club home game certainly sealed the idea of an anniversary publication.

Also, Steven Hutton and Peter Goodman at HR Media deserve a great deal of credit for helping to pull the whole thing together. Their writing and organisational expertise has been an invaluable contribution and helped bring all the pieces of information, memories and pictures into the book before you.

I hope you enjoy reading about Sheffield FC and our prestigious history in football.

Richard Tims
Chairman, Sheffield FC

Hall of Fame

A number of well-known names and figures from the world of football and beyond have enjoyed an association with Sheffield Football Club, both on and off the field.

Charles Clegg.

William Clegg.

THE TWO most prominent figures, Sir Nathaniel Creswick and William Prest, were especially vital to the development of the club and, as such, earn themselves a separate chapter later in this book.

From Sheffield FC's early days, **Sir John Charles Clegg**, once described as the 'Napoleon of Football' is undoubtedly the most famous player, achieving great things during his career.

Clegg played in the first ever international when England drew 0-0 against Scotland on 30 November 1872 in Glasgow. He was arguably with Sheffield at the time of the game, although during this period many players turned out for a number of teams. Clegg, for example, also played for the Wednesday.

In 1882 Sir Charles, as a referee, took charge of both the FA Cup Final and an England-Scotland game. He was also elected to the Football Association Council and by the end of the decade had become chairman. In 1923 he supplemented his role by becoming president until his death in 1937.

His brother, **William Edwin Clegg,** also featured for Sheffield FC and both played in Club's first FA Cup tie in 1873.

William reached international level, enjoying two appearances for England, the first when they beat Scotland 4-2 on 8 March 1873 and also against Wales on 18 January 1879.

Another Sheffield player, **Thomas Heathcote Sorby,** joined Clegg in the win over Wales. It was Sorby's only appearance for England, despite scoring in the 2-1 victory at the Kennington Oval in London.

According to the Football Association, it was by far the smallest crowd for any England match, kept low by a snowbound pitch. Reports range from 85 to 300 people in attendance.

From Sheffield FC's 1904 Amateur Cup winning side, **Fred Houghton Milnes** was a full-back who went on to represent an England amateur team which enjoyed a 15-0 romp against France at the Parc des Princes in Paris on 1 November 1906. The fact that the England goalkeeper only touched the ball twice gives an indication of their dominance.

Milnes was also responsible for taking the first football touring side to America. The team was named the Pilgrims and toured the US and Canada in 1905, 1909 and 1913. More details of the tours can be found later in this book.

Fred also assisted in the formation of the United States Football Association in 1912 and gave a trophy to encourage football in the schools of Yale and Harvard.

Sheffield FC's **Rev. John Robert Blayney Owen** was also capped by England in an international friendly with Scotland on 7 March 1874. England lost 2-1 in front of 7,000 spectators in Glasgow.

A Club player who enjoyed a more successful appearance for the national side was half-back **John Hudson** who captained England to a 7-0 win over Ireland in a Home Championship game on 24 February 1883, at Aigburth Park Cricket Club Ground, Liverpool.

Hudson also appeared for the Wednesday between 1880 and 1883, and played in the first match for Sheffield United FC against Club in August 1889. He died in November 1941.

William Henry Carr played in goal for England on 6 March 1875, in a 2-2 draw against Scotland at the Kennington Oval. It turned out to be his only game for England. He arrived 15 minutes late for his debut and in the days of no substitutions, William became the first international to play less than 90 minutes of football.

William is another player to have represented at least two clubs at one time, turning out for Owlerton as well as Sheffield FC. The goalkeeper was also selected for a Sheffield representative side which beat London 3-1 at Bramall Lane on 2 December 1871.

A key figure in the creation of Sheffield FC was **Harry Waters Chambers**, a former player who succeeded William Chesterman to become the club's third honorary secretary. He held the position for 22 years, during which he played in every Club game apart from four.

Chambers, who lived at Parkfield House, Highfields, was key to the development of the English Football Association and was the club's representative at its first meeting in October 1863.

The Chambers family enjoyed a link with Sheffield FC which lasted until 1950. Harry's son, Ernest, was a defender in the team which won the FA Amateur Cup in 1904 and Harry's other sons, Harry Junior and Geoffrey, both served as Club Presidents.

*One of Sheffield FC's most best-known players, **Harry Waters Chambers**.*

Looking back at individuals who have enjoyed long service with the club, it would be wrong not to give a mention to **H. B. Willey**, who spent 35 years as a player, secretary and finally President.

He became a director of Sheffield United and vice-president of the Sheffield and

Hallamshire County Football Association. In later years, he formed one of the best regional leagues, the Amateur Alliance, along with a Mr D. Jackson.

Mr Willey was known as 'The Club.' The respect he commanded was indicated by the minutes of a Club meeting on 6 December 1933, recording his death – 'for many years he carried the club on his back, administratively and financially, making up a yearly deficit from his own pocket.'

Thomas Edward Vickers was one of the founder members of Sheffield FC in 1857 and grandson of the founder of Naylor Vickers, a firm that began at Millsands and later established River Don Works.

Thomas, who in 1857 saw his father Edward become the first President of the Sheffield Chamber of Commerce, devoted a good amount of time to the Hallamshire Volunteers and was a keen football enthusiast who helped establish Hallam Football Club with another Sheffield FC member **John Charles Shaw**.

Shaw was born in Penistone in 1830 and probably exerted some influence on the playing rules adopted during those initial years.

He continued playing until well into his fifties and was referred to in the press as 'the gentleman who wouldn't grow old.' Shaw captained a team of veterans against a Sheffield FC side on 16 March 1885 and was described by a newspaper reporter as "playing admirably" despite his side's 5-1 defeat.

He was known as "an ardent sportsman whether in football or athletics who only lost two races in his life, played two hours of football, hunted with the harriers and walked home ten or twelve miles."

A Sheffield Collegiate friend of Creswick's, Shaw

H.B. Wiley. Former player, secretary and President of Sheffield FC during 35 years with the club.
(official SFC centenary book)

also became one of the town's most respected referees. When Sheffield played a London side in 1871, the visitors were a man short, but Shaw volunteered to play in goal.

He became vice president of Sheffield FA when it was founded in 1867, eventually becoming president from 1869 to 1885 – a time when the local association had an influential role in the national game.

In more recent times, some of the famous names to turn out for Sheffield FC include England internationals **Emlyn Hughes** and **Tony Currie**, with both wearing the famous red and black strip towards the end of their illustrious playing careers.

Neil Warnock played with Sheffield FC during the 1960s and **John Pearson**, former Sheffield Wednesday striker, enjoyed a relatively good spell as manager having been a player for the club.

Danny Bergara was manager of Sheffield FC during the 1983/84 season. He also had spells on the coaching staff at Sheffield Wednesday, Sheffield United and Rotherham United.

A recent initiative set up by Sheffield FC chairman Richard Tims has been club membership, which is proving to be a successful way to generate funds and also helping to raise the profile of the oldest club in the world.

Many illustrious names have become members, including FIFA President **Sepp Blatter**. Ever since the football chief signed up as a member, after Tims visited Paris to receive the FIFA Order of Merit, Mr Blatter has taken a keen interest in the club.

Former England manager **Sven Goran Eriksson** became a member of Sheffield FC while he was leading the national side.

Sheffield's **Michael Vaughan**, England's inspirational Ashes winning cricket captain, was pleased to join the oldest club, despite his well-known devotion to Sheffield Wednesday!

Former England head coach **Sven Goran Eriksson** also agreed to give his support to Sheffield FC when he was in charge of the national team. Sven has won Swedish, Portuguese and Italian league championships, as well as leading England to three quarter finals in major tournaments.

Sven told the Club website. "I am delighted to be a member of the oldest football club in the world. English football is rightly famous around the world for its rich history and heritage, and Sheffield FC is a big part of that history. I wish the club every success in the future."

From the world of music, Sheffield rock legends **Def Leppard** were presented with a team shirt and an early club photo by chairman Richard Tims after becoming members of the club.

Def Leppard's Joe Elliott added: "The picture is amazing. Sheffield FC should be a national treasure. It is something everyone should be proud of."

Bass player Rick Savage says: "What the club is trying to achieve is great. I hope it gets the recognition it deserves. Sheffield FC is an important part of football history."

Sheffield rock legends **Def Leppard** are one of the latest well-known names to become members of the club.

Football Seeds Sewn in Greenhouse

Little did anyone realise at the time but the humble little greenhouse in the Park district of Sheffield was nurturing not only tomatoes but also the seeds of a football club that was to become a universal phenomenon.

FOR IT was there that a group of Sheffield sports lovers laid the foundations of Sheffield FC, the world's first football club and an international beacon for all that was to follow in the next 150 years as the game spread to all four corners of the globe.

Sheffield FC's contribution to the sport is arguably one of the most famous football stories of all time, simply because of its tremendously influential significance. Many of today's features, such as the crossbar and the corner kick, had their roots in Sheffield and it is a matter of great pride that the city is regarded by many as the 'home' of modern football.

And, bearing in mind its place in the scheme of things, it is hardly surprising that the greenhouse, owned by Mr Asline Ward and used as the club's original headquarters, has become something of an important symbol reflecting the early

days of the club and the lasting achievements of its founder members.

It will always stand as a reminder of those tentative, early steps which turned into a strident, confident march as football found its feet and eventually conquered the world.

The painting Joe Scarborough has produced for the club which features the green house.

In the Beginning

It is generally accepted that the initial development of the modern game of football took place in England in the early and middle years of the 19th century. This modern form was developed from existing folk games – loosely organised local contests often held irregularly, usually between teams of unequal size – primarily by the boys of the major English public schools of Eton, Winchester, Harrow, Charterhouse, Westminster, Shrewsbury and Rugby.

THERE IS some evidence that a further form of organised football, independent of public school influence and based around public houses, existed, though it seems likely that the groups involved exerted far less influence on the development of the game than those who had attended the public schools and universities.

It is important to remember that in 1857, when Sheffield Football Club was formed, the game itself comprised of many loosely connected varieties spread across the whole country. Association football did not exist until the formation of the London-based Football Association in 1863 and, although there was a unique game-form known as rugby football, this was largely confined to Rugby School itself.

Despite the fact that the differing forms were commonly referred to as 'football', there is strong evidence to suggest that from around the 1830s two distinct types were beginning to emerge – the Rugby game which stressed handling, carrying and 'hacking' and the Eton Field Game, from Eton

A trophy presented to the winner of the running wide jump in Sheffield FC's Athletics Sports event in 1870.

College, which allowed handling only to stop the ball, and outlawed carrying and 'hacking' altogether. It is possible to claim that the latter was an early form of the association or soccer style and, certainly, the Sheffield game more closely resembled the Eton Field Game than that from Rugby School.

The first clubs formed specifically with the sole intention of allowing their members to play the newer forms of football on a regular basis were founded around the middle of the nineteenth century. While the majority were begun in and around London many were initiated in the Sheffield region. Indeed, by the mid-1850s organised football on a limited scale was being played there and the district boasts the existence of the world's oldest recorded footballing organisation, Sheffield Foot Ball Club (SFBC).

Sheffield FC Athletics Sports goblet presented in 1865 to the winner of the 150 yard run.

The club was designated as 'Foot Ball' in its constitution of 1858, probably emphasising the difference between ball games of the time which accentuated the use of the foot as opposed to the hand. Interestingly Sheffield was still known as a Foot Ball Club as late as 1869. The use of this title in 1858 offers further evidence that the game around this point was diverging into early soccer and rugby forms and helps explain the Sheffield area's preference for the former. Sheffield FC was formed on 24 October 1857 with the first written signs of a constitution and set of regulations appearing in autumn 1858.

There have been suggestions that the organisation was actually founded as early as 1855 and there is interesting evidence to support that as the year of the formation. Firstly, the club is listed in the original entries for the first FA Amateur Cup in 1893-4 as 'Sheffield 1855'. Secondly, when the team was victorious in that same competition in 1904, on presenting the trophy, Charles W Alcock of the FA noted that 'when it [Sheffield FC] was formed in 1855, there was no other club existing in England '. Thirdly, Richard Sparling, in his book *Romance of the Wednesday*, which was originally published in 1926, clearly mentions that 'Sheffield Club is the oldest existing football club in the world, and the minute-books go back to 1855'.

In his 'Note to Readers' he acknowledges the valuable assistance of J.C. Clegg, the famous Sheffield football administrator and one would be somewhat surprised to hear that such an eminent personage would have erred on the important date of formation. Interestingly, Sparling was the reporter who wrote an article in the *Sheffield Telegraph* (Wednesday 29 September 1954), specifically mentioning the missing minute books. He quoted the long-serving secretary HB Willey as saying, 'I used to have the minute book for 1855, but it was borrowed and never returned.'

It seems probable that some football was being played on a relatively regular intra-club basis in Sheffield by 1855. However, Sheffield Club only appears to have taken on a more permanent form in 1857. There is no conclusive evidence for believing there was any kind of real structure to proceedings before that date.

There have been misleading claims from teams outside of Sheffield to the title of 'oldest football club'. Certainly teams existed within the confines of academia – that is at schools and universities – which pre-dated 1857. For instance, Rugby School pupils issued a set of football rules as early as 1845, to which their counterparts at Eton responded with a set of essentially opposite laws two years later. The undergraduates and academics of Cambridge University were most prolific in legislating for the game. Five separate sets are at present known to have been issued:

Between 1838 and 1842, with Edgar Montagu, a former pupil at Shrewsbury School being a prime instigator;

In 1846, by John Charles Thring and Henry De Winton, also from Shrewsbury School;

In 1848, under the chairmanship of Henry Charles Malden;

In 1856, a copy of which still resides at Shrewsbury School and in St. John's College library in Cambridge;

And finally in 1863, perhaps the most important set which was used by the Football Association as the basis for their second laws which were distinctly anti-Rugby.

However, the presence of those schoolboys and undergraduates at the various institutions depended not upon their desire to play football but on educational requirements. Indeed, at the point of formation of Sheffield FC the cry, still heard today, of 'Come on, Club!' indicated the need to distinguish the first *clubs* from their *school* counterparts.

It is also important to reiterate that no club or school could have played *association* football before the formation of the Football Association in October 1863. Indeed, in the organisation's early years few clubs outside the London area employed the laws of the FA.

Early Days

The announcement of the 1858 AGM went as follows:

'The general annual meeting of the Sheffield Foot Ball Club will be held at my office on Thursday next at 7 o'clock for the purpose of appointing a committee and for other objects connected with the club.'

Nathaniel Creswick (Hon. Sec.) 9 East Parade, Sheffield, 9 October 1858.

The first committee comprised the following members:

President: Frederick Ward; Vice-Presidents: TA Sorby, J Ellison; Committee: W Prest, T Pierson, W Baker, JK Turner, TE Vickers; Honorary Secretary and Treasurer: N Creswick.

The two key names in this list are Nathaniel Creswick and William Prest, as both are acknowledged as the co-founders of Sheffield Football Club.

It has been suggested that Creswick and Prest decided to write to each major public school requesting a set of rules, using the preferred points of each to decide on a set of regulations for Sheffield. However, though public school influence was present, it was by no means direct. That is, it seems unlikely that either of the founders or early members had been educated at or brought the game directly from one of the major schools.

Doubt has been cast on the extent and importance of public school influence in Sheffield and it is difficult to refute the claim that few if any of the original members of the club had attended public schools. However, it is possible to disagree with any suggestion regarding the total lack of public school influence on the original rules. Surely one clue lies in an addition to the rules made in 1861-2. The inclusion of a 'rouge', at that time a peculiarly Eton Field Game differential scoring practice, must indicate some form of diffusion from that institution.

Percy Young, in his otherwise excellent book *Football in Sheffield*, is incorrect to claim the direct influence of an Old Etonian master at Collegiate School. Alfred Ainger did indeed teach there between the years 1864-6. Unfortunately he had not attended Eton and Young appears to have confused him with an ex-Etonian, Arthur Campbell Ainger, who had no connection with the Sheffield establishment.

One of the most intriguing questions that sociologists and historians concerned with the diffusion of football frequently ask is one regarding the adoption of a particular form of the game, whether it be a kicking and dribbling code or one involving handling and hacking, by the players of a specific geographical area. A possible hypothesis for the Sheffield area points to three main strands or avenues of diffusion:

Firstly, the type of football played by the boys at the local Sheffield Collegiate School would have been significant and they would have transferred these preferences when deciding on a code for Sheffield FC in 1857. Interestingly a game played on 14 March 1863 appears to illustrate the division

Continue page 18 ▼

An early Sheffield FC team photo, possibly from the 1890s.

The first playing rules

A decision was reached on 21 October 1858 when the Sheffield FC committee codified its game as follows. There is a good deal of deletion in the original text and the first draft is noted in square brackets following the final copy:

1. Kick off from the middle must be a place kick.
2. Kick out must not be from more than 25 yards out of goal.
3. Fair catch is a catch from any player provided the ball has not touched the ground and has not been thrown from touch. Entitles a free kick.
[Fair catch is a catch direct from the foot of the opposite side and entitles a free kick]
4. Charging is fair in case of a place kick (with the exception of a kick off as soon as the player offers to kick) but he may always draw back unless he has actually touched the ball with his foot.
5. No pushing with the hands is allowed but no hacking or tripping up is fair under any circumstances whatsoever.
[No pushing with the hands or hacking or tripping up is fair under any circumstances whatsoever]
6. Holding the ball, excepting the case of a free kick, is altogether disallowed.
[Knocking or pushing on the ball is altogether disallowed. The side breaking the rule forfeits a free kick to the opposite side]
7. No player may be held or pulled over.
8. It is not lawful to take the ball off the ground (except in touch) for any purpose whatever.
9. The ball may be pushed or hit under any circumstances.
If the ball be bounding it may be stopped by the hand (not pushed or hit) but if rolling it may not be stopped except by the foot]
10. A goal must be kicked but not from touch nor by a free kick from a catch.
[No goal may be kicked from touch nor by a free kick from a catch]
11. A ball in touch is dead, consequently the side that touches it down must bring it to the edge of the touch and throw it straight out from touch.
12. Each player must provide himself with a red and dark blue flannel cap, one colour to be worn by each side.

There is little doubt therefore in which camp the early protagonists of South Yorkshire placed themselves. Despite limited use of hands, a practice which was fairly widespread in most if not all football games at the time, the Sheffield Rules disallowed any excessively violent behaviour amongst participants by legislating quite clearly against hacking and tripping (Rule 5).
Holding the ball (Rule 8) was only allowed when making a 'fair catch', thereby preventing any carrying of the ball, which along with hacking, were the central features of the Rugby code.

Thos Pierson.

RULES, REGULATIONS, & LAWS

OF THE

SHEFFIELD

FOOT-BALL CLUB,

A LIST OF MEMBERS, &c.

PRESIDENT:

FREDERICK WARD, ESQ.

VICE-PRESIDENT:

T. A. SORBY, ESQ. | M. J. ELLISON. ESQ.

COMMITTEE:

T. PIERSON, ESQ. | S. NEWBOULD, ESQ.
W. PREST, ESQ. | G. MOSELEY, ESQ.
F. FOWLER, ESQ, |

HON. SEC. & TREASURER;

N. CRESWICK, ESQ.

1859.

RULES AND REGULATIO[NS]

FOR THE GOVERNMENT OF

The Sheffield Foot Ball Clu[b]

ESTABLISHED 1857.

1. That this Club be called the Sheffield Foo[t] [foot] ball Club.

2. That the Club be managed by a Committee of five Members, and the Officers of the Clu[b] three to be a quorum) to be elected at the An[nual] [An]nual General Meeting.

3. That the Annual Meeting of the Club shall [be] held on the Second Monday in October in each [yea]r, for the purpose of electing officers for the [ens]uing year, and for other purposes connected [with] the Club.

4. That the Committee shall be empowered to [call a] Special General Meeting of the Members of [the Cl]ub, on giving seven days' notice by circular [to each] Member specifying the object for which

---

4

such meeting is called. The discussion at such Special Meeting shall be confined to that object alone. The Committee shall also call a like Special General Meeting of the Members of the Club on the written request of any six members.

5. That the Club consist of honorary and playing Members.

6. That each honorary Member, on his admission to the Club, shall pay 5s. for the current year, and that the annual subscription of 5s. shall be due on the first day of November in each year.

7. That each playing Member on his admission to the Club shall pay 2s. 6d. subscription for the current year, and that the annual subscription of 2s. 6d. shall be due on the first day of November in each year.

8. That the Committee shall have power to make a further call on the playing Members in addition to the annual subscription, if they shall deem it necessary for the purposes of the Club, such further call not in any case to exceed the sum of 2s. 6d. in any year.

9. That retiring Members give notice in writing to the Hon. Sec. on or before the first day of October in any year.

10. That during the Season the Committee shall meet once in every fortnight for the dispatch of business.

LAWS

FOR THE GUIDANCE OF PLAYING MEMBERS.

1. Kick off from middle must be a place kick.

2. Kick out must not be from more than 25 yards out of goal.

3. Fair Catch is a catch from any player, provided the Ball has not touched the ground, or has not been thrown direct from touch, and entitles to a free kick.

4. Charging is fair in case of a place kick (with the exception of a kick off) as soon as the player offers to kick, but he may always draw back, unless he has actually touched the Ball with his foot.

5. Pushing with the hands is allowed, but no hacking or tripping up is fair under any circumstances whatsoever.

6. No player may be held or pulled over.

7. It is not lawful to take the Ball off the ground (except in touch) for any purpose whatever.

A LIST OF MEMBERS.

Appleton John, Glossop-road.
Aveling James H., M.D., Eyre-street.
Baker William, Sandon-place.
Belk Charles, Eccles-all-road.
Bingham J. E., Broomgrove.
Blackwell G. H., Sharrow.
Bonifant R. H., Sharrow.
Branson J. H., Broomgrove.
Broombead B. P., George-street.
Butcher Wm., jun., Endcliffe.
Cadman W. J. S., Handsworth Grange.
Cartledge Benj., Market-street.
Chambers, H. W., Parkfield House.
Corsan W. C., Leavy Greave.
Creswick A. J., Easthill.
Creswick N.,   ,,
Creswick W.,   ,,
Cutler J. E., The Laurels.
Dixon John, Endcliffe.
Dixon J. W. jun., Highfield House.
Ellison M. J., Norfolk Cottage.
Fairburn Robt., Paradise-square.
Favell Chas., Norfolk-street.
Favell J. N.,   ,,   ,,
Favell Thos.,   ,,   ,,
Favell W. F.,   ,,   ,,
Flockton March., Glossop-road.
Fowler Fredk., Wadsley Hall.

11

[But]ler Robt.. Parliament-st, Westminster.
[?]uiss Henry, Whirlow House.
[?]d Chas., Paradise-square.
[?]d Thos., jun., Wilkinson-street.
[?]d Wm.,
[?]y. H., Kiveton Park.   ,,
[?]ly C. H. B., Gell-street.
[F]rancis, Handsworth.
[?]n Henry, Sharrow.
[?] J. G., Priory Villas.
[?] Edward, East Cliff.
[?] Henry, jun., St. James'-row.
[?] Sharrow.
[?] W., Woodside.
[?]n., Glossop-road.
[?]hard, Shrewsbury Works.
[?]ry, Victoria Park.
[?] Bath Buildings.
[?]hn, Whiston.
[?]hn, Sharrow.
[?]muel, The Mount.
[?]on, Sharrow.
[?] Westville House.
[?]s,
[?]ray's Inn, London.
[?]l-street.
[?] Gray's Inn, London.
[?]am Cottage, Hallam-gate.
[?]inton-place.
[?] Boston.
[?]k-row.
[?]-street.
[?]orks, Eyre-street.

5

11. That the Season commence on the first Saturday in November and end on Easter Eve in each year.

12. That the Play Day of the Club be Saturday, from Two o'Clock until dark.

13. That the Season be closed by a variety of Athletic Sports, to be arranged and managed by a Committee to be appointed at a meeting of the Members in the month of January in each year.

14. That no one be eligible to contend in any of the sports unless he shall have been a Member of the Club for at least two months previous, and shall have played with the Club three times during the Season; but that the Sports Committee be empowered at their discretion to dispense with the latter part of this Rule in cases where the absence of any Member shall have been unavoidable.

15. That every Candidate for admission to the Club shall be proposed by one Member and seconded by another; his name and usual place of residence having been given to the Secretary, the proposer and seconder each subscribing his own name. The Candidates to be ballotted for by the Committee according to the priority of their nomination.

16. No ballot shall be valid unless three Committee-men vote, and two black balls shall exclude.

6

17. That all disputes occurring during play be referred to the Members of the Committee present on the ground; their decision to be final.

18. That the Officers for the Season 1859-60 be—President, Frederick Ward, Esq.; Vice-presidents, Thomas A. Sorby, Esq., and M. J. Ellison, Esq.; Committee-men, Thos. Pierson, W. Prest, Fredk. Fowler, S. Newbould, and G. Moseley; Honorary Secretary and Treasurer, N. Creswick.

19. That each Member shall have the privilege of introducing one or more friends in company with himself during each season. If residing within six miles of Sheffield such friends shall be introduced once only.

20. That the Committee shall take immediate cognizance of any infringement of these rules; and it shall be their special duty in case any circumstance shall occur likely to endanger the stability, or to interrupt the harmony and good order of the Club, to call a General Meeting in the mode above described; and in the event of two-thirds of the Members present at such meeting deciding by ballot on the expulsion of any Member, such Member shall cease to belong to the Club.

21. That these Rules, together with the Laws relating to the playing of the game, a list of the Members of the Club, and of the Sports of the preceding years, with the names of the winners of

7

the different events, be forthwith printed, and afterwards as often as the Committee shall think fit, and one copy sent to each Honorary Member. Playing Members to be charged a reasonable price for each copy they may require. Such price to be fixed by the committee each year.

12

Shortridge J., The Wicker
Simpson H., Wilkinson-street.
Smith Charles, M.D., Surrey-street.
Smith C. E., Fir Vale.
Smith George, Eldon-street.
Smith J. S., Portobello House.
Sorby T. A., Park Grange.
Staniforth S., Broad-lane.
Streatfeild R. B., Broomhall Park.
Swift S. C., Broomgrove.
Swift Frederick, „
Tarpley K. M., Leeds.
Tennant Robert, Endcliffe.
Turner B., East Bank.
Turner J. K., Glossop Road.
Turner Thomas, Aldwark.
Turner W., Bushire.
Turton Thomas, Clarkhouse Road.
Turton T. J., „
Vickers A., Tapton Hall.
Vickers F., „
Vickers T. E., „
Walker Herbert J., Paradise-square.
Ward Frederick, Norfolk Road.
Wass Allen, Broomgrove-terrace.
Webster Henry, Market-place.
Webster W., Jun., Shirley.

16

The Prize for being second in three Events on the 5th April, 1859, was awarded to Mr. Flockton.

The above Sports took place in the Field of the Club at East Bank, which in consequence of the previous rain was on both occasions in a very unfavourable state.

Events.	Winners. 1858. April 4.	1859. April 5.
Flat Race, 100 yards	W. Prest.	
" 120 yards (winner of 100 yards race previous year barred)		J. E. Bingham. (15 seconds.)
Standing Wide Jump	W. Prest. (8ft. 10in.)	W. Prest. (9ft. 8in.)
Walking a Mile		H. Bonifant. (8min. 58sec.)
		R. H. Bonifant. (9min. 45sec.)
		W. Prest. (64 sec.)
	Henry Miller. (22ft. 9in.)	T. E. Vickers. (23ft. 2in.)
	Chas. Flockton. (7 sec.)	
	W. Prest. (ft. 11in.)	W. Prest. (5ft. 2in.)
	Prest.	A. Vickers.

Events.	Winners. 1858. April 4.	1858. April 5.
...mer (14lbs.)	W. Prest. (47ft. 8 in.)	
(12lbs.)		
		T. E. Vickers. (66ft. 6in.)
...p	W. Prest. (36ft.)	W. Prest. (36ft. 9in.)
...ble	W. Prest.	W. Prest. (25½sec.)
		W. Jepson.
...e (150 yards		
...ards over 1...		
...le, 100 yds		

	Winners. 1858. April 4.
...ing a Cricket Ball	J. H. Branson. (82yds. 2ft. 6in.)
...le Race	N. Creswick. (6min. 2sec.)
... High Jump	W. Prest.
...Race, 80 yards	W. Prest.
...ic' of Football	Wm. Gould.
...ce (200 yards over 12 hurdles)	W. Prest

Images from Sheffield FC's rule book of 1859, which includes the winners from the Athletics Sports Events in 1858 and 1859. This is the first printed football club rule book in the world.

Pawson and Brailsford, Printers, High-st.

of the club at that time between old boys of Sheffield Collegiate and others educated elsewhere. The game between eleven Old Collegians and an equal number of other members of the club was played at East Bank.

The Collegians, who included Nathaniel Creswick, two Vickers, Waterfall and Chambers won by 'three or four goals to one.' The method of scoring used in this game – 'goals' rather than 'tries' – suggests an embryo soccer rather than rugby form. Whilst it remains unclear what constituted their favoured form of the game, it is noteworthy that the school was still playing under Association rules at least until 1880 and probably beyond. Secondly, the officers of Sheffield FC almost certainly wrote to certain of the major public schools for their football rules or were at least familiar with elements of their codes. As previously mentioned, the eventual adoption of the Eton Field Game practice of the 'rouge' provides evidence for public school influence.

Finally, the exponents of local forms of folk or mob football – in this case particularly those living in the nearby thriving football enclave of Thurlstone and Penistone, where a kicking and dribbling form of the game thrived – would probably have attempted to shape the final code of rules to their liking.

At Sheffield FC's Jubilee dinner in 1907, Col. Nathaniel Creswick commented about how he and Prest had written to the leading public schools in the country to enquire as to what their rules were.

"And what a lot of different rules we received," said Creswick. "I remember one rule, I believe from Winchester, which was that you should not hold and hack a man at the same time.

"The number of players and the hours of play in those far-off days were unlimited. We generally played until it was dark."

John Charles Shaw, a subsequent president of the Sheffield FA, joint founder of Hallam FC and a former member of Sheffield FC, was born in Penistone in 1830 and would probably have exerted some influence on the playing rules adopted during those initial years.

Annual Athletic Sports

These annual events appear to have been almost more important to the members than games of football. There may have been several reasons for this. Firstly there was, in the late 1850s, a distinct lack of footballing opponents in and around Sheffield. Although the members would have played matches against each other – first half of the alphabet versus second half, married against single – these would have become monotonous and the urge to compete against others would have been strong.

Secondly, the athletics may well have been an instrument for raising money and an important social gathering. It remained a one-off event in the club calendar rather than a weekly or monthly affair which regular football fixtures would have constituted.

The relationship between football and athletics inaugurated by Sheffield FC, can be seen with the

Thomas Vickers was one of the founder committee members of Sheffield FC and his father Edward was the first President of the Sheffield Chamber of Commerce in the same year. This is John Singer Sargent's Portrait.

number of clubs with Athletic or Athletic Football Club in their name.

Events included:

1858 – Flat race, standing and running, wide jump, walking a mile, putting the stone, running and standing high jump, backwards race, throwing a cricket ball, mile run, hopping race, longest kick of football, hurdle, wrestling, throwing the hammer, hop-skip-jump, sack race.

The 1858 event took place at East Bank and was graced by the presence of a great number of ladies and gentlemen, the elite of the town and neighbourhood.

The following table indicates the occupations of the club's members in 1858 and 1859.

Occupations of the members of Sheffield FC for the seasons 1857-8 and 1858-9

(Many thanks to Adrian Harvey for allowing the inclusion of this table)

Occupation	1858	1859
Architect	1	1
Brewer	1	1
Dentist	1	1
Doctor	2	1
Gentleman	1	1
Joiner	1	1
Land agent	2	2
Manager	1	1
Manufacturer	7	8
Merchant	6	8
Reverend	1	2
Silver plater	1	0
Solicitor	8	8
Spirit seller	1	1
Stationer	1	0
Superintendent	1	1
Surgeon	3	4
Veterinary surgeon	1	1
Wine merchant	1	1
Unknown	18	35
Total	59	78

A Club for an Elite

Sheffield FC appears to have offered membership to 'gentlemen' only and for many years seems to have remained a socially exclusive organisation. Indeed, the club originally came into existence to provide recreation for 'The Young Gentlemen of Sheffield' and for many years were referred to as the 'Gentlemen' by their opponents. The local press was supportive of this view. A report in the *Sheffield Daily Telegraph* noted that 'The club enjoys a prestige not possessed by any of its now many rivals, and numbers amongst its members and friends the *élite* of the town and neighbourhood' (9 May, 1865).

Two years later the same newspaper commented that 'A good deal of the prestige of the club is due to character of the members', continuing that 'The club holds the premier position amongst the athletic clubs of the town; its members are almost exclusively of the middle class; and its patrons and supporters include most of the leading men in the neighbourhood.' (7 May 1867).

Certainly in the context of the hierarchy of social stratification in the city, the initial officers of the club are probably best described as upper class or upper middle class.

The President, Frederick Ward, was to become Chairman of Sheffield Forge and Rolling Mills Limited; the Vice-President, T.A. Sorby, was a well-known local merchant in his family's business; J. Ellison, the other Vice-President, was also a successful merchant; W. Baker was a technologist and local intellectual; whilst T.E. Vickers graduated to become Master Cutler in 1872 and was heavily involved as commanding officer of the local Hallamshire Volunteers.

Two letters from W.F. Beardshaw attempting to persuade players to represent the club give a further indication of the relationship between Sheffield FC and its neighbours.

A painting of an early football game.

To: A Sorby (Cambridge)

Dear Sir,

We are drawn against Sheffield Heeley in the second round of the National Cup and are to play them at Bramall Lane on 26th if possible. This match is of special importance and we must win it **under any circumstances** as it will seriously lower the prestige of our club if we are beaten by any local team.

I sincerely trust you will put aside all other matters and give us your assistance upon this occasion. We must also have Pawson's help and I would ask you to second our efforts in procuring him if necessary.

W.F. Beardshaw – 11 November 1881.

Heeley were victorious by four goals to nil. Two Sorbys represented Sheffield – R.A. Sorby in goal and C.E. Sorby in defence.

Another such communication from Beardshaw dated 16 September 1884 asking for playing assistance from a gentleman by the name of J. Jeeves finished with the sentiment, 'remember we are the only strictly amateur club in the north.' This is interesting, as professionalism in football was not legalised by the FA until July 1885 and it would seem from Beardshaw's sentiments that the distinction between amateur and professional was, in some quarters, already being drawn.

Creswick and Prest The inventors of club football

Over the many years of its existence many people have been involved in the development of Sheffield FC – but none can quite match the influential roles of Nathaniel Creswick and William Prest.

BOTH ARE generally acknowledged as being the co-founders of the oldest club in the world and during their involvement with Sheffield FC helped to bring together powerful figures from the city to establish the club as a significant voice in the football community.

Nathaniel Creswick was born on 31 July 1831 in Park Field, Sheffield, as the son of a prosperous silver-plate manufacturer also named Nathaniel. The Creswicks were an old Sheffield family who had lived in the area since the 14th century and had premises in the Pepper Alley near Fargate.

Nathaniel was educated at Sheffield Collegiate School, a Church of England institution catering for local middle class boys, from April 1839 to June 1847. He progressed to become a solicitor and also Chairman of Joseph Rodgers and Sons Limited, a local silver-plate company.

His name was prominently associated with the volunteer movement, which he served for more than 40 years working hard to inaugurate the 4th Yorkshire West Riding Volunteer Artillery – better known as the Hallamshire Rifles.

Creswick retired with the rank of Colonel and in 1897 was presented with the honour of Civil Companion of the Bath in recognition of his services as a volunteer. In his obituary in the *Sheffield Daily Telegraph* on 22 October 1917, his work with the Rifles was described as 'the most notable public interest in Sir Nathaniel's life.' His services for the volunteer force were further recognised in 1909 when he was awarded his knighthood.

Away from the Hallamshire Rifles, Creswick was an all-round sportsman, being a pedestrian – a term used to describe walking races – a runner, cricketer and footballer.

In 1860 Creswick was also awarded a medal by the Royal Humane Society after showing great personal valour when he saved a youth from drowning.

Thomas Bardwell was skating on a dam near Crookes in the city when the ice broke at a deep part of the water. Creswick threw the man a piece of wooden fencing but Bardwell was too weak to hang on and so Nathaniel crept onto the ice and seized the man by the collar to stop him sinking further.

Unfortunately the ice collapsed under their combined weight and both plunged into the water. Creswick managed to grip the ice with one hand while holding the man with the other and

William Prest.

Nathaniel Creswick.

eventually other rescuers threw them a wooden gate which they were able to cling to and both were dragged clear.

William Prest, who lived nearby, provided a change of clothes for Creswick. The latter was praised for his coolness, presence of mind and courage in a difficult situation. So impressed were the onlookers that a public subscription was opened immediately following the rescue and a suitably inscribed silver salver to the value of over fifty pounds was procured for Creswick.

Creswick married Sarah Ann Walker in 1866, his wife originating from York, the same city as Creswick's good friend Prest. It might be interesting to speculate whether Prest and Sarah were previously acquainted.

Creswick was ten years older than his wife and the couple had two children, a boy, Francis, and a girl, Ethel. In the 1891 Census they are listed as living at 7, Maugerhay, Norton Green on the outskirts of the city and interestingly not far from the club's current stadium in Dronfield. They were sufficiently wealthy to have a cook and a housemaid.

Creswick's good friend William Prest was born to William and Arabella Prest on 1 April 1832 in York.

In 1850, his father John Prest purchased the old established wine business of John Porter and Sons, which was eventually taken over by William's brother, John Beevor Prest, initially trading under the title Porter and Prest.

In the mid-1850s William joined his brother and the firm became JB and W Prest, Wine Merchants, 46 High Street, Sheffield. Following the death of his brother John, William was in sole charge until joining forces with E.C. Vinen of London.

Initially William lived on Collegiate Crescent in Sheffield, near to Collegiate School, but at his death he resided at Dam Cottage on Crookes Road to the west of the city. He had, in fact, lodged there for many years and appeared in the 1861 and 1881

census returns at that address and was consequently close by to aid Creswick in his heroic ice rescue.

Prest was a versatile sportsman playing both cricket and football and gained an early reputation as a very fast runner.

In cricket he was described as an outstanding left-handed batsman and the quickest and most brilliant fielder in local cricket.

He was present at the meeting which formed the Sheffield United Cricket Club in 1854 and played for Yorkshire in 16 cricket matches from 1852 to 1862, captaining the team as well as being selected for an all England XI.

Wisden records William playing 28 innings scoring 280 runs, at an average of 10.21 and his best bowling figure were three for 69.

He played in the first public event at Bramall Lane on April 30 1855, a cricket match made up players from six of leading cricket clubs.

Prest, a member of Sheffield Cricket Club and on the committee of Sheffield United Cricket Club, became the first cricketer at Bramall Lane to be out without scoring when J Rowbotham bowled him.

At Sheffield FC's first annual athletics event at East Bank on 4 April 1858 more than 4,000 people were in attendance. Prest distinguished himself by achieving no fewer than twelve first prizes, including the 100-yard dash, five jumping contests, throwing the hammer, heavyweight wrestling, sack race, hopping race, hurdles and the backward sprint!

In 1859 William was involved, along with Creswick, in the formation of the 2nd West Yorkshire (Hallamshire) Rifles, better known as simply the Hallamshire Rifles. He was appointed Adjutant of the Battalion and later rose to become a Lieutenant Colonel, though he never actually commanded the regiment.

An enthusiastic and keen politician, Prest was a Conservative but according to his obituary notice in 1885, 'however strong might be his feelings in these matters he was never accused of being an offensive politician'.

William Prest had an older brother, Edward,

who attended Uppingham School and Cambridge University (1843 – 1847) and was thus probably familiar with football as it was played in those institutions at that time.

At Cambridge, Edward was a direct contemporary of John Charles Thring, one of the framers of the university football rules for 1846. Thring was actually at the same college, St. John's, as Edward Prest and even shared the same tutor. Thring himself was a true football missionary, who held a dislike of the rugby form of the game and issued his own football rules, called "The Simplest Game", in 1862. This significant and previously undiscovered information may partly explain why Sheffield football resembled the future association game as the Cambridge University model consistently leaned towards a kicking and dribbling style, being distinctly anti-Rugby in form.

William died on 10 February 1885, aged 52, after suffering a sudden and fatal seizure following a ruptured blood vessel. He was buried with full military honours.

His obituary appeared in the *Sheffield Daily Telegraph* the following day. It stated that Prest suddenly collapsed 'within a few paces of his own office'. He had been unwell for a year and had been advised to stay at home, but such was his commitment to the local Hallamshire Volunteers that he insisted in helping with plans for a ball to be held for the officers of that group.

His funeral took place three days later at Sheffield General Cemetery and thousands lined the route. There were so many present that a letter of complaint appeared in a local newspaper complaining at the damage done to other graves in the cemetery by the large assembly of mourners.

Despite Prest's interesting past, it seems likely that Creswick was probably the more influential of the two men and there is evidence to support this in the offices ascribed to them when the club was formed.

Creswick was appointed Honorary Secretary and Treasurer, whilst Prest merely served on the committee. It also seems likely, therefore, that during discussions over the framing of the first rules, Creswick, along with the others present, would have brought to bear their previous experiences of, and preferences for, particular forms of football. However, it would almost certainly have been the Honorary Secretary/Treasurer who exerted the most influence.

At Last...
Teams to Play!

It was three years after their own foundation when Sheffield Football Club had local rivals to play against in the form of Hallam FC. Hallam became the first team to develop from an existing cricket club, a route subsequently followed by Sheffield Wednesday and Sheffield United.

HALLAM CRICKET CLUB was established in 1805 and by 1859 they had no less than 300 members. They were initially known as the Hallam and Stumperlowe Club, the latter part of the title being included out of courtesy towards several members of the team who resided in the nearby hamlet of that name.

Founded by Thomas Vickers and John Shaw, who had both been members of Sheffield FC, Hallam played its first game against Club at its Sandygate ground on Boxing Day 1860.

The game is thought to be the first ever recorded football match between two different clubs. A *Sheffield Daily Telegraph* report on Friday 28 December 1860 described the unique event, as Sheffield FC opposed Hallam and Stumperlowe Club:

'This match was played on Wednesday upon the Hallam cricket ground in the presence of a large number of spectators. Owing to the severe weather several players were absent from each side, but the spirit exhibited by those who were present prevented the game from flagging or becoming uninteresting to the observers, who were extremely liberal with their plaudits on the successful "charge" or quiet "dodge", and equally unsparing in their sarcasm and country "chaff" on the unfortunate victims of the slippery ground or the "pure" scientific.

'The day was beautiful and the uniform of the men contrasting with each other and the pure snow had a most picturesque appearance. The Sheffielders turned out in their usual scarlet and white, whilst most of the country players wore the blue garment of the Hallam Club. It would be invidious to pick out the play of any particular gentleman when all did well, but we must give the palm to the Sheffield players as being the most scientific and also more alive to the advantage of upsetting their opponent.

'No serious accidents however occurred – the game was conducted with good temper and in a friendly spirit – and when darkness closed upon the scene, the Sheffield Club, notwithstanding their inferior numbers, counted two goals to nothing, and went home fully satisfied with their victory.'

The play of several members of the Sheffield team against Hallam is described as being 'scientific', the reporter perhaps alluding to the skilful play of a more experienced team. This may have included team as well as individual patterns of play, something that might be associated with a combination honed from several years of playing together.

There was even a cricket match between the two football rivals played at Bramall Lane on 29 August 1862. Amongst those playing for Sheffield were Nathaniel Creswick, William Prest and William Chesterman, whilst Hallam's team included William Waterfall, two other members of the Creswick family and John Shaw.

Sheffield FC and Hallam have retained their fierce rivalry since that historic Boxing Day game. One of the best remembered clashes was on 29 December 1862 when the first ever football match took place at Bramall Lane after the ground's Committee of Management allowed the game to be played on their hallowed cricket pitch.

However, despite the match being a friendly in aid of the Lancashire Distress Fund, a particularly violent incident took place.

The following match report from the *Sheffield and Rotherham Independent*, dated 3 January 1863 notes the local enmities and the growing seriousness of the game, which appears to have been reflected in the participants' behaviour.

'Football match at Bramall Lane – On Monday the Sheffield and Hallam football clubs played a match at Bramall Lane cricket ground, the proceeds being devoted to the Lancashire distress fund. The Hallam party having won the toss, played with the wind in their favour, but, at "half-time", having failed to score, the ends were changed.

'After a rest of 15 minutes, play was resumed. The great expectation seemed to be that Sheffield, with the wind now in their favour, would soon get a goal. The Hallam men, however, played with great determination and successfully defended their goal.

'They appeared to have many partisans present and when they succeeded in "downing" a man, their ardent friends were more noisily jubilant.

'At one time it appeared likely that the match would be turned into a general fight. Major Creswick (Sheffield) had got the ball away and was struggling against great odds – Mr Shaw and Mr Waterfall (Hallam). Major Creswick was held by Waterfall and in the struggle Waterfall was accidentally hit by the Major. All parties were agreed that the hit was accidental. Waterfall, however, ran at the Major in the most irritable manner and struck him several times. He also threw off his waistcoat and began to "show fight" in

An early Sheffield FC team photo.

earnest. Major Creswick, who preserved his temper admirably, did not return a single blow.

'They were surrounded by partisans and for a few minutes there was every appearance of a general fight amongst players and spectators. The advice of older and cooler heads at length prevailed, the field was cleared and play again resumed. At 3 o'clock the play terminated in a "draw", there being neither a goal nor a rouge scored by either party.

'The conduct of Waterfall was much condemned and several of the Hallam players expressed their deep regret at the occurrence. There were a few, however, who seemed to rejoice that the Major had been hit and were just as ready to "Hallam it" on the slightest provocation. The cry was very general that Waterfall should be expelled from the field, but, though this extreme course was not taken, he was quietly placed as goalkeeper for the short time the play continued.'

The following reply from the Hallam players was published in the *Sheffield and Rotherham Independent* three days later:

'In the early part of the game Waterfall charged the Major on which the Major threatened to strike him if he did so again, for which the Major afterwards apologised.

Later in the game when all the players were waiting the decision of the umpires on a rouge, the Major very unfairly took the ball from the hands of one of our players, and commenced kicking it towards their goal, when he was met by Waterfall who charged him and the Major deliberately struck Waterfall on the face, which Waterfall immediately returned.'

The Hallam Players

Further accounts of Sheffield v Hallam encounters serve to confirm the highly competitive nature of these early local rivalries. The previously men-

Robert Cross, butcher, Pickering, to Sarah, eldest daughter of Mr. G. Case, Scarborough.

On the 24th inst., at Eckington, by the Rev. E. B. Estcourt, Mr. Wm. White, Grantham, to Curtis, youngest daughter of Mr. Shacklock, grocer, Eckington.

DIED.

On the 27th inst., Mr. Isaac Read, scissor manufacturer, in his 71st year.

On the 27th inst., Mrs. Lucy Storey, widow, Carver-street, in her 84th year.

On the 22nd inst., Mrs. Mackenzie, of Holly-street, aged 65.

LOCAL & GENERAL INTELLIGENCE.

SHEFFIELD FOOTBALL CLUB *v.* HALLAM AND STUMPERLOW CLUBS.—This match was played on Wednesday upon the Hallam cricket ground in the presence of a large number of spectators. Owing to the severe weather several players were absent from each side, but the spirit exhibited by those who were present prevented the game from flagging or becoming uninteresting to the observers, who were extremely liberal with their plaudits on the successful charge or quiet "dodge," and equally unsparing in their sarcasm and country "chaff" on the unfortunate victims of the slippery ground or the "pure" scientific. The day was beautiful and the "uniform" of the men contrasting with each other and the pure snow had a most picturesque appearance. The Sheffielders turned out in their usual scarlet and white, whilst most of the country players wore the blue garment of the Stumperlow club. It would be invidious to single out the play of any particular gentleman when all did well, but we must give the palm to the Sheffield players as being the most scientific and also more alive to the advantage of upsetting their opponents. No serious accidents however occurred—the game was conducted with good temper and in a friendly spirit—and when darkness closed upon the scene the Sheffield club, notwithstanding their inferior numbers, counted two goals to nothing, and went home fully satisfied with their victory.

MR. W. WILLOTT'S SERIO-COMIC OPERATIC ENTERTAINMENT.—It will be perceived from the advertisements that our former townsman, Mr. William Willott, has just embarked in a new musical entertainment, which is to be given to-morrow (Saturday) and Monday evenings, in the music hall, Surrey-street, under the most promising auspices. Mr. Willott has secured the valuable services of Madlle. Lancia and Mr. Augustus Braham, both of whom are distinguished amongst the principal operatic artists in the metropolis. The lady has long studied her arduous profession in the best Italian schools, and Mr. Augustus Braham is a worthy son of the renowned tenor whose reputation has always stood unrivalled in this country for the execution of a certain class of music which is again about to be introduced to us through the medium of the present entertainment. "The Bay of Biscay," "Oft on a stilly night," and other ballads equally popular, are included in the programme, while the music entrusted to the vocal powers of Madame Lancia is of that pure and graceful character which could only be successfully rendered by an *artiste* well skilled in the science. In addition to the more classic part of the performance, there is to be an agreeable admixture of mirth and humour, for the mastering of which Mr. Willott will himself exercise the best of his ability. Mr. Willott has long been well known here in a very different capacity, and we trust that the good opinion he has won in this town will be strengthened by the result of this new venture. If report speak truly (and there can be no reason to think otherwise) the entertainment well deserves a large share of public patronage, as well on the ground of its intrinsic merit, as on that of the "good name" attached to the performers.

A FIREMAN KILLED AT KNOTTINGLEY.—On Wednesday night last a fatal accident happened at Knottingley, near Pontefract, on the Lancashire and Yorkshire line, to a fireman in the employ of the company. The deceased was on the engine of a goods train going south from Wakefield. On coming out of the station yard at Knottingley, and when about to get on the main line, the engine ran off the line and down the embankment rolling upon and killing the fireman in its fall. The driver escaped,

March ..	.. 305	.. 4 800	.. 4·889	.. 6 650	.. 4·625
April.... 1·820	.. 3·140	.. 6·940	.. 1·570	.. 3·235	.. 3·030
May .... 2·310	.. 1·570	.. ·445	.. 3·245	.. 1·100	.. 4·965
June .... 3·160	.. 3·105	.. 4·025	.. 5·495	.. 3·895	.. 3·920
July .... 4·025	.. 3·445	.. 2·075	.. 2·040	.. 4·400	.. 3·860
Aug..... 1·915	.. 6·930	.. 7·355	.. 6·130	.. 2·055	.. 2·435
Sept. .. ·870	.. 3·165	.. 4·780	.. 3·105	.. 3 025	.. 3·575
Oct. .... 6·400	.. 2·760	.. 4·150	.. 4·505	.. 1·460	.. 5·375
Nov. .... 1·045	.. 2·305	.. 3·310	.. 3·665	.. 4·040	.. 0·960
Dec. .... 2·135	.. 1·455	.. 3 180	.. 3·440	.. 2·355	.. 3·095
Total ..28·775	..36·060	..46·155	..44·280	..37·940¼	..40·060

FOOTBALL.—MILTON v. MACKENZIE.—On Saturday last, a match was played at Cremorne Gardens between the above clubs, which, after a very exciting game, resulted in the Mackenzie gaining one goal and one rouge to Milton's one goal.

FOOTBALL—A match at this popular game was played at Pitsmoor on Saturday, between second elevens of the Pitsmoor and Sheffield clubs. Enough of spirited play was exhibited on both sides to satisfy the most ardent lookers on, who, as well as the players themselves, seemed to enjoy this healthful and exciting old English game. The Pitsmoor club was victorious, scoring one goal and two rouges against the Sheffield one goal and one rouge.

FOOTBALL MATCH AT BRAMALL LANE.—On Monday, the Sheffield and Hallam football clubs played a match at the Bramall lane cricket ground, the proceeds being devoted to the Lancashire distress fund. With the exception of a few slight showers the weather was all that could be wished, and there was a very fair number of spectators. The Hallam party having won the toss, played with the wind in their favour, but, at "half-time," having failed to score, the ends were changed. After a rest of fifteen minutes play was resumed. The general expectation seemed to be that Sheffield, with the wind now in their favour, would soon get a goal. The Hallam men, however, played with great determination, and successfully defended their goal. They appeared to have many partisans present, and when they succeeded in "downing" a man, their ardent friends were more noisily jubilant. At one time it appeared likely that the match would be turned into a general fight. Major Creswick (Sheffield) had got the ball away, and was struggling against great odds— Mr. Shaw and Mr. Waterfall (Hallam). Major Creswick was held by Waterfall, and in the struggle Waterfall was accidentally hit by the Major. All parties are agreed that the hit was accidental. Waterfall, however, ran at the Major in the most irritable manner, and struck at him several times. He also threw off his waistcoat and began to "show fight" in earnest. Major Creswick, who preserved his temper admirably, did not return a single blow. They were surrounded by partisans, and for a few minutes there was every appearance of a general fight amongst players and spectators. The advice of older and cooler heads at length prevailed, the field was cleared, and play again resumed. At three o'clock the play terminated in a "draw," there being neither a goal nor a rouge scored by either party. The conduct of Waterfall was much condemned, and several of the Hallam players expressed their deep regret at the occurrence. There were a few, however, who seemed to rejoice that the Major had been hit, and were just as ready to "Hallam it," on the slightest provocation. The cry was very general that Waterfall should be expelled from the field, but though this extreme course was not taken, he was quietly placed as goal keeper for the short time the play continued. We hope the Hallam players will set themselves right by making the amende honourable, for it is not to be endured that healthful sports should degenerate into unseemly brawls. We understand that many of the Sheffield players deprecate the long interval in the middle of the game, that was ..ted to refreshments.

tioned Thomas Vickers recalled games between the two in which "Bull strength" was the principal feature. He noted seeing the ball 'laying quietly on the ground whilst yards away opposing players were blocking, ramming and butting each other.'

Sheffield Football Club's William Clegg also recalled an incident against Hallam as follows:

'Down one side of the field there ran a stone wall only a foot or so off the touch line. I was running down the wing with the ball and after me came hurtling a great big fellow, twice my weight. I swerved quickly to one side and he went smack against the wall with such force that he knocked several stones out of position!'

Whilst Sheffield held athletic sports to end their season, Hallam instituted the 'Great Steeplechase'. This event was held for the first time on 4 October 1862 and stretched over a ten-mile course from the club's ground at Sandygate around the Rivelin Valley.

The rivalry between the two clubs continues to this day with both teams still retaining their original colours of Sheffield red and Hallam blue. Many football fans have flocked to encounters at Hallam's Sandygate ground to see competitive fixtures between the two teams. Most view Sandygate as the oldest football club ground in the world and the game as the oldest club fixture in football.

On 26 December 2006 both teams met in the Northern Counties East League Premier Division – 146 years to the day since the first ever game. The match finished with Sheffield again the victors, this time earning a 3-1 victory.

Within five years of Sheffield FC's birth there were fifteen clubs registered in and around the city, including teams such as Norfolk, Fir Vale and Heeley.

Nathaniel Creswick once recalled a game played at Sheffield barracks saying, 'It was originally agreed to play 20-a-side, but after we had been playing for some time I thought there were too many on the opposite side. I asked the captain of the soldiers' team to parade his men and count them. He did so, and it was found there was 38 of them.'

Interest in 'the beautiful game' soon increased with more and more teams being formed. Sheffield Wednesday were one of these clubs and began life in 1867. When Sheffield United were established 22 years later, it was Sheffield FC who provided the opposition for their first game, United winning 3-1 at the Ecclesall Road ground in August 1889.

With football firmly established in South Yorkshire, Sheffield FC began to spread the football gospel out of their own area and their first fixture away from their familiar surroundings took place in Nottingham on 2 January 1865. Both teams consisted of eighteen players and lined-up as follows:

Sheffield: N. Creswick, A.J. Creswick, H.W. Chambers, A.A. Dixon, Jnr. Shaw, J.C. Shaw, B. Shepherd, C. Appleton, A.M. Wild, F. Knowles, W. Turton, A. Wightman, J. Wild, R. Favell, H. Cadman, G.H. Hawksley, A. Earnshaw and W. Chesterman.

Nottingham: J. Patterson, A. Simons, C. Daft, Bignall, Elliott, J. Wright, Moody, Elliott, Flack, Hodges, Gibson, Allott, Smith, Deeds, Scrimshaw, Rastall, Parker and B. Bradley.

The game was played under Nottingham rules and lasted for three hours, with Sheffield winning 1-0.

Club continued with their proselytising efforts outside Sheffield, with games against Glasgow and two further matches each against Nottingham Forest and Lincoln in 1865. However, the most significant games were those to be played against London.

An early group shot ahead of an inter-city association game between Sheffield and Glasgow, in Glasgow.

Sheffield, London and the Football Association

Sheffield FC can have some claim to have been involved in the initial development of the Football Association (FA).

A T THE first meeting of the London body on 26 October 1863 at the Freemason's Tavern, Sheffield's representative appears to have been Harry Waters Chambers. While the main delegates were listed assiduously, the FA minutes of the initial gathering noted that 'there were several other gentlemen present interested in the subject, who, although players, did not definitively represent any club.'

In Sheffield FC's centenary publication, there is a mention of three other gentlemen who also acted as fellow representatives of the Club at the meeting – G. Allcock, A.W. Willis and J. Morton. A player by the name of J. Morton is listed as playing for the Sheffield Football Association against the Birmingham Football Association on 20 January 1876.

The four individuals only attended as observers. However, Sheffield FC, after some discussions between members, did decide to become a member of the FA a month after its formation.

The next communication between Sheffield and the FA was brought to the attention of delegates at the FA's fifth meeting on 1 December 1863. It was at this point that discussion about the difference between kickers and handlers – association football and rugby – essentially took place.

The minutes note that there was a lengthy communication from William Chesterman, then Honorary Secretary of Sheffield FC.

Chesterman enclosed a subscription but delivered a stinging rebuke to the London law-makers by offering the opinion that Law 9, allowing running with the ball, and Law 10, allowing hacking, were opposed to football and more suggestive of wrestling.

Below is his letter in full:

Dear Sir,
Our committee have read with great interest the late discussions respecting the laws of football and believing the association now formed is likely to promote the game, they are anxious to enroll the club amongst the list of members and I herewith enclose the amount of subscription.

We think it very desirable a general code of laws should be established and heartily wish you success in the undertaking. I enclose a copy of our rules and perhaps you will excuse a few remarks on them.

I am very much in favour of a crossbar. Without one it is sometimes very difficult for an umpire to decide and, whatever his decision, he generally displeases someone. In your Rule 5, I think the ball, when thrown or kicked back into play, should be not less than six yards [Chesterman is referring to the distance at which an opposing player should be allowed to stand]. *If thrown less, it is very liable to go out again at first kick.*

We have no printed rule at all like your No. 6 [Offside], but I have written in the book a rule which is always played by us. Nos. 9 and 10 [Running with ball and, amongst other robust, rugby-like actions, hacking] are, I think, directly opposed to football, the latter especially being more like wrestling. I cannot see any science in taking a run-kick at a player at the risk of laming him for life.

Your No.14 will be altogether new to our players I suppose the idea is that nails are dangerous. We strictly prohibit spikes, but though it is the general custom in this neighbourhood to wear nails, I have never yet heard of an accident resulting from the use of them.

I think our No.15 (which we have only had about two years) a very useful and desirable rule and worth your consideration [This was the rouge, a differential scoring method]. Doubtless the foregoing are all old arguments but I thought that perhaps they would not be uninteresting on showing how the game is played in this neighbourhood.

On hearing that we are accepted as members, I shall be glad to appoint representatives to attend your meetings.

Yours Truly
W Chesterman
Hon. Sec. Sheffield Football Club, Sheffield
November 30, 1863

With the formation of the Football Association – essentially an organisation of London-based clubs – in autumn 1863, the game seemingly possessed a focal point for further promotion.

However, with the split between the kickers and the handlers over the exclusion of hacking – indiscriminate kicking of opponents – and tacitly running with the ball, the London body had 'shot itself in the foot' and suffered from the defection of the Blackheath teams who favoured the Rugby form.

Strangely, the FA seemingly ignored the vibrant Sheffield footballing sub-culture. This is doubly perplexing as, firstly, Harry Chambers had acted as one of Sheffield FC's observers at their initial meeting and would presumably have been known to them. Secondly, the South Yorkshire community could have provided comforting support for the nascent, besieged FA.

Despite the differences, it fell to Chesterman to initiate meaningful contact with the FA by suggesting a contest between the two bodies.

This was discussed and accepted at the FA Committee meeting held on 22 February 1866 when it was suggested that members of the London clubs should put forward nominations of players for the fixture.

Although Sheffield were members of the FA, it had always been agreed that they would retain a large degree of autonomy and still play by their own set of laws.

In Sheffield FC's records, Chesterman notes that he 'did not propose for the Sheffield clubs to play the association but our club'. Sheffield's selection was not a truly representative side as it only consisted of players from Sheffield FC. This may further strengthen the view that Sheffield FC at that point thought of themselves, probably quite correctly, as an elite body in the city and illustrates the FA's confusion over the organisation of football in Sheffield.

The match between London and Sheffield was played on 31 March 1866 at Battersea Park with the home team winning by two goals and four touchdowns to nil.

The fact that the fixture was played under FA rules probably assisted the London combination. The game itself was reported as 'a very hot one, although Sheffield were over-matched, many of the Londoners were badly knocked about.'

It was in this game where the London team first witnessed Sheffield players heading the ball – a sight never seen before in the south of the country and one which caused some laughter.

A return match was mooted but disagreements over rules prevented one being arranged. Sheffield had offered to play the rules according to whoever

FOOTBALL MATCH,

WANDERERS, London, v. QUEEN'S PARK,

Played on Hampden Park, Mount Florida, Glasgow, on Saturday, 9th October, 1875

H. W. CHAMBERS,
Goal Keeper

A. H. STRATFORD,
Back.

A. F. KINNAIRD,
Right X Half-back
Blue and white cap

W. S. RAWSON
Left X Half-back
Blue cap

J. TURNER,
Left X Wing

W. D GREIG,
Right X Wing
Blue stockings

R. L. GEAVES,
Centre X Red and white cap

C. W. ALCOCK,
Captain X and Centre.
Cap— blue and white chequers.

H. S. OTTER,
X Centre Park cap

HUBERT HERON,
Left X Wing
Grey stockings, and orange, violet and black cap

J. KENRICK,
Right X Wing
Cerise and French grey cap

UMPIRE—ROBERT GARDINER, CLYDESDALE CLUB
REFEREE—THOMAS HASWELL 3RD L.R.V. CLUB
UMPIRE—W. C. MITCHELL, QUEEN'S PARK CLUB

HENRY M'NEILL,
Left X Front
Orange and black stockings.

W MACKINNON,
Centre X Front
Red stockings.

JAMES B. WEIR,
Right X Front
Red and white stockings

M. M'NEIL,
Left X Back-up
Blue and white stockings.

C. HERRIOT,
Centre X Back-up
Black and white cap—no stocking.

THOMAS LAWRIE,
Right X Back-up.
White stockings

JAS. PHILIPS,
Left X Half-back
Red and black stockings.

CHAS. CAMPBELL,
Right X Half-back
Red, white, and black stockings.

R. W. NEIL,
Left X Back.
Heather mixture stockings

JOSEPH TAYLOR,
Captain and X Right Back
Black and white stockings.

JOHN DICKSON,
Goal Keeper.

Colours : Wanderers, White Jersey — Queen's Park, Black and White Stripe.
Play will begin at 3.30 p.m, and end at 5 p.m.

PLEASE DO NOT STRAIN THE ROPES.

AN INTERESTING PROGRAMME OF A MATCH IN 1875. THE PLAYERS WERE DISTINGUISHED BY THEIR VARIETY OF APPAREL, INCLUDING, IN SOME CASES, THE WEARING OF CAPS. IT WILL BE NOTED, TOO, THAT THE FORMATION OF THE WANDERERS' TEAM IS QUITE DIFFERENT TO QUEEN'S PARK

Harry Waters Chambers surprisingly played goal for London Wanderers against Queen's Park, due to a lack of a goalkeeper. Although he was substituted soon after kick-off after a poor start.

was the home team, but this was declined by the London Association who felt that as they were formed with the object of creating a universal code of rules, it would be ill advised to have a team playing to rules set by another club.

Lack of enthusiasm for the FA reached its lowest ebb by early 1867 when only six representatives, including Chesterman, attended one of their meetings held on 12 February.

At this point, 15 clubs were playing the game in Sheffield compared to the ten teams affiliated to the FA. The latter body appears to have possessed few missionary qualities and its members appeared content to have formulated a code by which diverse teams could play each other.

With this task completed, there was even a suggestion that the FA might disband. However, Sheffield still appeared subordinate to the FA. This was particularly evident when Chesterman, at this point still representing the Club, attempted but failed to amend four FA laws – two concerning the use of the rouge (a differential scoring method), one regarding offside and another relating to the use of hands. All of his motions were defeated.

As the number of clubs in Sheffield began to grow, the Sheffield Football Association was formed in 1867. It was only at this time that a closer relationship between the FA in London and Sheffield started to develop.

It was, however, five years after the first game between Sheffield and London that the next fixture between the two associations was played. The FA's Honorary Secretary, C.W. Alcock, captained a team of London-based players which travelled to South Yorkshire.

Unfortunately Alcock had managed to bring only ten men on the journey north. But J.C. Shaw, then President of the Sheffield Association, offered to help make up the numbers by playing for the visitors.

The game took place at Bramall Lane, Sheffield, and the local eleven reversed the first game's result by winning 3-1. By this time the team was a truly representative team, comprising players from several different clubs from across the city.

After the contest the *Sheffield and Rotherham Independent* commented on how successful football in the city had become, writing: 'This healthy and exhilarating game has gradually advanced in public favour since the introduction of it into this neighbourhood by the Sheffield Club some years ago. Until at the present time it is quite as popular in the winter as cricket is in the summer with the sport-loving population of Sheffield.'

Games between Sheffield and London continued, with 15 taking place between the two teams over the next four years. As the two associations competed against each other on the field, friendships between individuals undoubtedly developed.

One noteworthy example of this was when the Wanderers Football Club of London, five times winners of the FA Cup in the 1870s, were struggling to find a goalkeeper for the long trip north to face Queen's Park in Glasgow.

Harry Waters Chambers came forward to assist his friend C.W. Alcock, captain of the London team. Unfortunately, it was to be an instantly forgettable experience for the Sheffield man. A reporter for the *Sheffield and Rotherham Independent* related:

'Three goals were got in the first 40 minutes by the Scotch eleven, after which Chambers, the English goalkeeper, was supplanted by Geaves, who acted more efficiently.'

The reporter confirmed in the team list that it was indeed H.W. Chambers of Sheffield.

Admiration for the London style of football progressed and in time the FA consolidated its position as the superior authority.

Significantly, the 1871-2 season saw the introduction of the FA Challenge Cup – a competition which was to gain recognition as one of the most famous club tournaments in the world.

Up for the Cup!

Sheffield FC first competed in the prestigious FA Cup competition in 1873-4 when it was in its third season but there was some confusion about their entry. It all seemed to arise out of a misunderstanding between the FA and their Sheffield counterparts as to the distinction between Sheffield FC and Sheffield FA.

MINUTES OF the national FA meeting of 20 August 1873 reveal the following: "A letter was read from H. Chambers entering the Sheffield Association for the cup competition. The secretary was directed to inform Mr Chambers that the entry could only be accepted upon the condition that it emanated from one of the clubs supporting the Sheffield Association, and not from the Association in its corporate capacity, and further that the club selected to represent the Association should play only bona fida members."

Presumably, the Sheffield FA selected Sheffield FC and they were drawn against another new entrant, Shropshire Wanderers, who were based at Shrewsbury.

The first game, at Bramall Lane on Thursday 30 October 1873, ended in stalemate, a 0-0 draw, and the home side included Chambers, Chesterman and the two Clegg brothers.

The replay, played on Shrewsbury Racecourse on Monday 17 November, was also a 0-0 draw and on this occasion neither W.E. Clegg nor Chesterman were playing.

The game was quite physical and the Wanderers' robust style resulted in the visitors playing the closing stages with only nine fit players.

The Wanderers also had the services of their captain, John Hawley Edwards who had not featured in the first game. A larger than life character, he was the first dual international, playing for England in 1874 and Wales two years later.

He was an FA Cup winner with the Wanderers in 1876 and was representing that club when he gained his Welsh cap in the same year. Taking everything into account, it is surprising that the Sheffielders held on but, thanks to the fine play of H. Sorby and J.C. Clegg, they forced a draw.

So, after two draws, how was the tie decided? A newspaper report noted: "After the match, the players dined together at the 'Raven' where it was agreed to toss which should be considered victorious and the Sheffield captain (Mr Chambers) won."

In the next round, played on Saturday 22 November, Sheffield FC met Pilgrims at Kennington Oval, winning by a single goal scored by H. Sorby. Chesterman and C.W. Alcock acted as the umpires.

Then, in the quarter finals, with seven teams

remaining in the competition and Swifts being given a bye, they faced another London side, Clapham Rovers.

To offset any prohibitive travel costs for one team, the two sides met at Peterborough which was approximately halfway between the two cities.

Sheffield were two goals down by half-time but narrowed the deficit with 20 minutes to go. Try as they might, however, they could not find an equaliser.

A reporter covering the match made several interesting comments. He bemoaned that "senseless regulation, the throw-in" which appeared to break up the rhythm of this particular game, although the weather did not help matters with a severe wind blowing across the pitch.

Sheffield played much of the match with only ten men and one of them was carrying an injury. Each player, no doubt because of their relatively high social status, was referred to in the newspaper report as 'Mr'.

The reporter finished his article in a rather acrimonious manner, stating: "Some rather curious decisions were given during the match which did not always appear to be quite unbiased. The play was particularly keen and there was more feeling imported into the match than is usually witnessed in such contests."

Interestingly, it is on record that in their early cup games, the Sheffield gentlemen wore kid gloves and carried a coin in their hands. This curbed any desire to handle the ball because, if they offended, club officials would penalise the offender by taking the coin from them.

Sheffield FC's FA Cup forays continued into the 1870s, 1880s and early 1890s. In 1875-6, they were again drawn against Shropshire Wanderers who scratched and in the next round opponents Upton Park also scratched.

It meant that Sheffield FC were through to round three without kicking a ball. Unfortunately their progress was halted at the Oval where they were beaten 2-0 by the Battersea, London-based Wanderers who went on to win the cup.

FOOTBALL.
SHEFFIELD CLUB v. SHROPSHIRE WANDERERS

The above match was played yesterday afternoon, at Bramall Lane Ground, in the presence of about 600 spectators. Our football readers will doubtless be aware that the London Association, with an idea of encouraging the game, have offered for competition a challenge cup, which has now been contested for two years, the Wanderers (London) having secured the victory in the final tie on both occasions, and have only to win the present season's series of matches to entitle them to the ownership. The match under notice was one of the first ties, and as it ended in a draw, and must be decided to allow of the winner to compete in the second round, it is more than probable that the Sheffield Club will proceed to Shrewsbury to bring, if possible, the match to a more satisfactory result. The ground was in very fair condition, and an improvement was noticeable in a goal line being marked the entire width of the ground, but in the interests of the players it is advisable to remove the cords and stakes on the upper side of the ground, as in the excitement of the play a serious injury might be sustained; one of the contestants yesterday—Mr. Ellison—being tripped up with the cord. The match was a capital one, the Shropshire men being a most even and plucky team, their dribbling being capital; whilst the Sheffield Club, on the contrary, were not so well represented as we have seen them. Play commenced about 2.40, and Sheffield having won the toss, their opponents kicked off towards Bramall lane. The first to show prominently was M. Ellison, and soon afterwards Dixon charged one of his opponents in a resolute manner. Good dribbling by W. E. Clegg preceded an excellent specimen of play by the Shropshire gentleman—Mr. O. Spencer. A good shot at goal by J. C. Clegg was of too lofty a nature to be successful, it going over the bar. Good dribbling by Wylie for Shropshire, and a good shot by Dixon, which just went outside the post for Sheffield, were worthy of note, when Wigfall landed one in the goal mouth, which was well stopped by the goal keeper. A scrimmage then occurred in front of the Shropshire goal, and so near was it of being successful, that the ball cannoned off the goal post. A back kick by J. C. Clegg was also dangerously near the visitor's territory. A capital run and charge by Ellison along the upper portion of the ground was acknowledged by the spectators with a hearty round of applause. A similar specimen by O. Spencer on the low side was worthy of a similar ovation. Up to this time the advantage of the play had been in favour of Sheffield, but the Wanderers now worked the ball past the enemy's half backs and placed the home stronghold in jeopardy; but the good keeping of H. F. Chambers proved equal to the occasion, and it was quickly returned to the centre of the field where W. E. Clegg got possession of it, and a kick by him went just outside the post. A heavy charge about this time so disabled Fretson, that shortly afterwards he had to retire, and his side laboured under the disadvantage of playing one short. Sorby—one of the Sheffield forwards—then executed a bit of pretty dribbling, and a good kick by Dixon, well stopped by the Shropshire goal keeper, preceded another capital run by O. Spencer. A fine specimen of dribbling tactics was then shown by W. E. Clegg. A good kick by Wylie just went outside the Sheffield goal, and a second by him landed over the cross bar. Half time had now elapsed, and as neither team had scored, ends were changed. Judicious "heading" by Dixon was noticeable, after which a capital kick into the goal mouth was only saved with great difficulty by the custodian, who, in stopping the ball, cannoned himself against the goal post. O. Spencer again distinguished himself for Shropshire by an excellent run, steering the ball past the goal keeper, having a clear course, but his final kick went outside the post. Another onslaught was then made on the Sheffield citadel, this time by Wylie, but it was too high, going over the cross-bar. J. C. Clegg now made another good back kick, and a couple of good scrimmages ensued in the Shropshire goal, but possession of the ball was obtained by F. Spencer, and he cleverly ran it to the Sheffield goal, but failed to effect the downfall of the stronghold. Some pretty dribbling by Sorby was then shown for Sheffield, and a good run by O. Spencer, whose last effort went over the cross-bar. Time was then called, the match ending in a draw, neither team scoring. In addition to those already mentioned T. Willey showed general play of a noticeable character. Players names appended.

Shropshire Wanderers: O. Spencer (captain), C. E. Wace, J. E. Wylie, H. Chapman, G. F. Thompson, S. C. Merie, F. Spencer, A. T. Ward, B. V. Randall, J. Denning, W. Dunn. Umpire, W. Matthews.

Sheffield Club: H. W. Chambers (captain), J. C. Clegg, W. E. Clegg, T. C. Willey, F. J. Fretson, W. Cheetham, H. Sorby, H. E. Dixon, M. Ellison, J. Willey. Umpire, F. S. Chambers.

y, Nov. 19, Thurgarton Priory 11 0
Friday, Nov. 21, Cropwell Butler 11 0
HIGH PEAK HARRIERS.
Saturday, Nov. 22, Aldwark Grange.......... 12 0
HALLAM AND ECCLESALL HARRIERS.
Wednesday, Nov. 19, Froggatt Edge 10 0
STANNINGTON HARRIERS.
Wednesday, Nov. 19, Dungworth..............
Friday, Nov. 21, Rivelin Mill....................
Monday, Nov. 24, Bradfield...................

FOOTBALL.
SHEFFIELD CLUB v. SHROPSHIRE WANDERERS.

The second match between the above two clubs took place on the Shrewsbury Race Course on Monday, in the presence of a numerous body of spectators, who were, however, rather partial in their demonstrations of approval. The first match, it will be remembered, was played at Bramall lane Cricket Ground, on the 30th of October, and, after a stubborn contest, ended in a draw. As it was one of the first ties for the London Association Challenge Cup it was necessary for a decision of some sort to be arrived at, and it was ultimately arranged that the Sheffielders should visit Shrewsbury. The cutlery town were scarcely so strongly represented as was anticipated, as Mr. W. E. Clegg is at present in London. Mr. J. R. B. Owen, who played so well in the recent London match, was unable to be present, and Mr. A. Kirke-Smith, for the same reason, was an absentee. The ground is perfectly level, and there was no wind; and although the Wanderers won the toss it was of no advantage. The match at once assumed a remarkably fast aspect, the Shropshire charging being difficult to withstand. M. Ellison was disabled, and after the match had to go to a surgeon; whilst shortly after half-time R. Wake had to retire, so that the Sheffield team were rather at a disadvantage. This superiority in numbers caused the Wanderers to have slightly the best of the play, particularly at the finish. The match ultimately ended in a draw, neither team scoring, a proof how evenly balanced the teams must be. After the match the players dined together, at the "Raven," where it was agreed to toss which should be considered victorious, and the Sheffield captain (Mr. Chambers) won. We should have specially mentioned the magnificent play of Messrs. H. Sorby and J. C. Clegg for Sheffield, and the almost marvellous skill of Mr. Hawley Edwards, the Shropshire captain. The Sheffield club in their second tie are drawn with "The Pilgrims," a metropolitan club, and the contest between them is arranged for Saturday next at Hackney, a fixture which clashes with Sheffield Club v. Notts., at Nottingham, on that date. The following are the names of the Sheffield team:—H. W. Chambers (capt.), J. C. Clegg, T. Willey, J. Willey, H. E. Dixon, H. Sorby, M. Ellison, J. Wigfull, C. Webster, R. Wake, and C. Vickers.

The Turf.

CITY BETTING.—TUESDAY.
CROYDON STEEPLECHASE.
100 to 12 agst Fantome, taken & off
14 to 1 — Dora, taken
14 to 1 — Silvermere, taken
14 to 1 — Congress, taken
16 to 1 — Alice Lee, taken
20 to 1 — Chimney Sweep, taken

BUCEPHALUS' WARWICK NOTES.

A crowded card proved the forerunner of a capital day's sport, the fields in every case being unusually

---

The *Illustrated Sporting and Dramatic News* wrote of Sheffield FC in 1874: "Football nowhere thrives more rapidly or is cultivated with more enthusiasm than in the town of keen blades, of armour plates, of monster factories and monster chimneys that belch forth never ceasing clouds of smoke."

1878 saw them reach round four where they were once more beaten by the Wanderers who were one of the leading amateur clubs of the time. Again the southern side emerged as cup winners that season.

Notts County proved to be something of a bogey side for Sheffield FC in 1884-5 and 1885-6, beating them 5-0 and 8-0 respectively.

There was an abrupt end to the club's FA Cup progress in 1890/91 season when, in qualifying round one, they were hammered 13-0 by Rotherham Town. However, it would not be too long before Sheffield FC had begun involvement in another prestigious cup competition – the FA Amateur Cup.

The club continue to play in the FA Cup to this very day, though they would need to win in the region of 13 games, including the qualifying stages, in order to reach the final!

Their best FA Cup run in recent times was in 2002/03 season when Sheffield FC reached the Fourth Qualifying Round of the FA Cup for the first time in over 40 years, bowing out to Conference side Northwich Victoria in a match played at Sheffield United's Bramall Lane stadium.

Sheffield – The Home of Football

As well as boasting the world's oldest football club, Sheffield has played a crucial role in developing the game we know and love today. The city pioneered many innovations in football during those early years and here we take a look at what Sheffield did for the sport.

FIRSTLY, SHEFFIELD FC players and officials can certainly be credited with pioneering the use of a crossbar rather than tape.

The club's secretary, William Chesterman, mentioned in his letter to the FA in 1863 that crossbars were already being used in Sheffield. He stated: "I am very much in favour of a crossbar, without one it is sometimes difficult for the umpire to decide, and whatever his decision, he generally displeases someone."

It was 12 years later before the crossbar was permitted, finally becoming obligatory over a length of tape between the posts, which was abolished in 1882.

Sheffield also led the way in penalising an offence with a free-kick to the opposition. As a consequence, opponents were forced to retire a certain distance from the restarts. Although Chesterman states that this distance was originally six yards, this is undoubtedly the forerunner of the ten-yard rule in the modern game.

At an FA committee meeting on 12 February 1867 Sheffield FC, again through Chesterman, offered two suggested law changes – one regarding offside and the other adding to an existing rule regarding restrictions on holding the ball or pushing it with the hands, thus further distancing the game from the rugby form.

While the suggestions were not accepted by the FA at the time, it was a sign of how forward thinking the club was in developing the game, with both rules now used in the laws of football.

Chesterman suggested: 'Rule VII to be expunged and substituted with: "Any player between an opponent's goal and goalkeeper, unless he has followed the ball there, is offside and out of play. The goalkeeper is that player in the defending side who, for the time being, is nearest to his own goal." Not carried.'

'Add to Rule XI: "Holding the ball, knocking or pushing it with the hands or arms is altogether disallowed and the side breaking this rule forfeits a free kick to the opponent's side." Not carried.'

One anecdotal story during the early years of the Club was that the players of Sheffield FC wore gloves with a coin in each hand. If they touched the ball with their hands the coin would be taken away from them by an official!

This account further strengthens the view that Sheffield footballers were determined to maintain

...nce... ...erently than on the occasion when they first met Nottingham, and to them the bowling of Barker had now lost its terror. Marsden's style of batting came into full exercise, and no less than 227 runs resulted from it. Sheffield won in a single innings.

THE FOOTBALL MATCH BY ELECTRIC LIGHT.

[FROM THE LONDON "TELEGRAPH."]

Inventions and improvements nowadays tread so quickly upon the heels of each other that timid people may well be pardoned if they become doubtful and anxious. No sooner do we hear that Mr. Edison has succeeded in dividing the electric light, and that another gentleman has given his name to the Jablochkoff "candle," than the report comes that football has been played in Sheffield at eventide, not by the aid of a ball covered with phosphoric oil, as our forefathers thought might some day be managed, but by turning night into noon, and making such a blaze by means of four "points" and a couple of steam engines that the ladies who were amongst the spectators were obliged to put up their parasols, and the players to shade their eyes. It is not too soon to ask where all this is to end, when we learn that even the moon, which shone out brilliantly, was "completely overpowered by the illumination," and are told that, "had it been brilliant sunshine, the play could not have been much better." The sad fact for those to note who cling to old customs is that the players of Sheffield took to this science-provided sport as naturally as though they had been born in electrical phenomena. We read how the sides were formed; how one goal was endangered and then another; how raids were made into the enemy's lines; how "Buttery had a corner kick," and "Bishop made a brilliant shot;" how there were "scrimmages," "neat runs," and goals won and lost; but not a word about the assemblage being stricken with awe at the sight of the luminaries which enabled them to enjoy all this fun. In ancient times such a performance, in a "soft, blue, clear light," would have been accounted positively wicked. The pious prelates of those halcyon days would never have permitted such a "defying of Providence" by football players or any other set of people. It is clear that we have nearly broken away from prejudice at last, and are almost prepared to acknowledge that after all it is an extremely simple and beautiful world, of which very much more might be made than has ever been attempted, if only a little thought were employed, and that, having once begun to recognise the possibility of anything, there is no need for further surprise. The unfortunate bird of which Lord Dufferin tells us, and which, observing in the Arctic regions the, to him, unaccountable phenomenon of an ever-present sun, crowed until at length he fell dead from the boom end of the vessel, weary of announcing a perpetual morn, had never been "educated up" to the marvels of nature. The good Sheffield folk are so far in advance of the bewildered cock that they are prepared to accept and make the best use of everything which science provides; and, as the new electric light, with its wonderful powers, comes before them, they utilise it for the sturdy game which Englishmen love so well.

The war balloon which escaped on Monday from Woolwich without any attendant landed on Tuesday morning in Essex.

SKIN GRAFTING.—The *Birmingham Daily Post* says:—We gave an account a few days ago of a case of accidental scalping successfully treated in America by skin grafting, and we suggested that Birmingham surgeons might profit by the hint. We have since heard, with pleasure, that the operation has lately been practised in Birmingham in a case of peculiar difficulty, and with complete and most gratifying success.

The new English church at Bia...

---

their stance in favour of the kicking and dribbling form of the game.

On the question of kick-off times, the founders of Sheffield FC agreed that, 'the play day for the Club be on Saturday from two o'clock until dark.' This is likely to be one of the first mentions of club football being a Saturday afternoon pastime, something which continues in England to this day.

With Sheffield FC's early football prestige, and the social standing of their players and administrators in the city, it is probable that their influence was strong. However, the Sheffield footballing community as a whole can also be credited with the introduction of other initiatives.

In 1868, the newly-formed Sheffield Football Association introduced the corner kick and goal-kick, four years before the FA accepted the rule on 17 February 1872. The new law, which is subscribed below, also features a mention of the previous introduction of the crossbar.

Rule VII: To erase and substitute with – "When the ball is kicked over the crossbar of the goal, it must be kicked off by the side behind whose goal it went, within six yards from the limit of their goal. The side who thus kicks the ball are entitled to a fair kick-off in whatever way they please; the opposite side not being allowed to approach within six yards of the ball.

> "When the ball is kicked behind the goal-line, a player of the opposite side to that which kicked it out shall kick it from the nearest corner flag. No player to be allowed within six yards of the ball until kicked."

The city's football administrators pioneered the Players Accident Scheme and in the 1866-67 season South Yorkshire clubs were the first to compete in a cup competition, the Youdan Cup. The final took place at Bramall Lane on March 5, with the trophy being provided by Tom Youdan, a local music hall manager.

The cup was won by Hallam who narrowly beat

Norfolk. Many years later the silverware went missing and was only recovered in 1997 when a Scottish antiques dealer acquired it and sold it back to the original winners.

The following season another theatre manager, Oliver Cromwell, offered a further cup for competition. The Cromwell Cup was won by Wednesday who, playing in their inaugural season, defeated Garrick in the final on 15 February 1868.

Sheffield officials were also the first to suggest the use of North v South trial matches for players in order to select national teams. The games originated from the Sheffield v London encounters during the 1870s.

One important football first was seen in the city on 14 October 1878 when the first game under floodlights took place at Bramall Lane, one of the most prominent sporting venues in the country.

The teams consisted of famous players from across Sheffield and the surrounding area, with each being captained by one of the Clegg brothers.

Players included the likes of Billy Mosforth and Jack Hunter, and several members of the Sheffield FC team. Essentially, the match was held to promote the new invention of electric light!

The *Sheffield Daily Telegraph* recorded the moment with a report of the game on 15 October 1878. Part of the report is reproduced below:

'The Sheffield public were last evening introduced to a decided novelty in football – a match with the assistance of the electric light. The contest, which took place at Bramall Lane Ground between two teams selected by the Sheffield Football Association, was the first ever played in this country – or anywhere else, we believe – with the aid of artificial illumination, especially of that which is derived from the powerful currents of electricity.'

This unique game attracted huge interest from the public with approximately 20,000 people attending.

The report added: 'The match was announced to commence at half-past seven o'clock and considerably before that hour the roads to Bramall Lane were completely besieged. The wonder was where all the people came from. There seemed no end to the ever-coming stream, and the crowd of excited people outside the gates struggling to pass in at the turnstiles created a scene of great animation.'

A colourful newspaper report on the occasion from the London *Daily Telegraph* focused entirely on this new phenomenon and rarely covered any part of the match.

Part of it read: 'No sooner do we hear that Mr Edison has succeeded in dividing the electric light, and that another gentleman has given his name to the Jablochkoff "candle," than the report comes that football has been played in Sheffield at eventide, not by the aid of a ball covered with phosphoric oil, as our forefathers thought might some day be managed, but by turning night into noon, and making such a blaze by means of four "points" and a couple of steam engines that the ladies who were amongst the spectators were obliged to put up their parasols, and the players to shade their eyes.'

The report further notes that 'the players of Sheffield took to this science-provided sport as naturally as though they had been born in electrical phenomena.'

It ended by saying, 'The good Sheffield folk are so far in advance…that they are prepared to accept and make the best use of everything which science provides; and, as the new electric light, with its wonderful powers, comes before them, they utilise it for the sturdy game which Englishmen love so well.'

The teams and officials were as follows:
Reds: F. Stacey, J. Houseley, J. Hunter, E. Buttery, F. Hinde, J.C. Clegg, W. Mosforth, A. Woodcock, C. Stratford, H.E. Barber, G. Anthony

Blues: T. Lawson, W.E. Clegg, R. Gregory, T. Buttery, W.H. Stacey, G.B. Marples, A. Malpas, J. Tomlinson, E.H. Barber, T. Bishop, P. Patterson
Umpires: W. Skinner, R.W. Dickinson
Referee: W. Pierce Dix

As the new sport of football began to gain popularity, players found the need to test themselves against opponents from far afield.

Sheffield was involved in one of the first England-Scotland city clashes. The initial encounter between the Sheffield Football Association and Glasgow Football Association took place on 14 March 1874 at Bramall Lane, Sheffield.

The game ended in a 2-2 draw and was witnessed by almost six thousand spectators. The Glasgow eleven wore their national colours of 'blue jerseys with the lion of Scotland on the left breast, white knickerbockers and various coloured stockings.'

All but one player from Glasgow played for the Queen's Park club, with the teams as follows:

Sheffield: J. Marsh (Captain), J.C. Clegg, J. Houseley, H.E. Dixon, W.H. Carr, J.R.B. Owen, W.H. Stacey, R. Gregory, J. Hunter, T. Buttery, W. Wilkinson.
Glasgow and District: J.J. Thompson (Captain), C. Campbell, J.B. Weir, W. Mackinnon, A. Mackinnon, H. McNeill, J. Taylor, R. Gardner, F. Anderson, J.H Wilson, D. Wotherspoon.

Two years later, in February 1876, Glasgow again visited Sheffield, this time winning by two goals to nil. The game was noteworthy because of the appearance in the Scottish eleven of James Joseph Lang, who would subsequently come to live in Sheffield to play for the Wednesday club.

He was almost certainly the first professional soccer player, receiving payment from Wednesday to turn out for them over several seasons.

The Scots generally dominated the fixture between the two cities, winning eleven of the first fourteen games. Sheffield's solitary victory came in February 1882 when, at home, they beat Glasgow 3-1.

Spectators were generally of the opinion that the football played that day was of the highest calibre ever seen in the city. Included in the Sheffield team was the great Billy Mosforth and future FA Cup winner Jack Hunter, along with future England international and Sheffield FC player John Hudson.

The fixture continued until 1938, with only a break for the duration of war, and did not resume until a single fixture in 1949. The series recommenced under floodlights in 1954.

The first fourteen results were as follows:

1874	Sheffield 2	Glasgow 2
1875	Glasgow 2	Sheffield 0
1876	Sheffield 0	Glasgow 2
1877	Glasgow 1	Sheffield 0
1878	Sheffield 2	Glasgow 4
1879	Glasgow 4	Sheffield 1
1880	Sheffield 0	Glasgow 1
1881	Glasgow 3	Sheffield 0
1882	Sheffield 3	Glasgow 1
1883	Glasgow 4	Sheffield 2
1884	Sheffield 1	Glasgow 2
1885	Glasgow 9	Sheffield 1
1886	Sheffield 2	Glasgow 2
1887	Glasgow 10	Sheffield 3

Finally, the administrators and players in football were becoming increasingly aware of growing commercial opportunities and, with South Yorkshire the first in England in which football was played in a relatively organised club form, it is perhaps not surprising that stories of emergent professionalism should emanate from Sheffield.

Amateur Cup Victory

It is now more than 100 years ago, but the day Sheffield FC won the Amateur Cup still stands out as one of the most important headlines in the pages of the city's illustrious sporting history.

It was without doubt the club's finest hour, surpassing all other on-the-field achievements and winning it became a recognition befitting its proud past.

THE FIRST Amateur Cup competition was staged in the 1893-4 season with Sheffield FC being instrumental in its initiation. With the gradual decline in both entry and success in the FA Cup due to the domination of the competition by professional clubs, amateur teams were in something of a dilemma in the early 1890s and the situation prompted the club to write the following letter to the Football Association:

> 'That this meeting of the Sheffield Football Club considers it in the interests of amateur football that a trophy should be offered by the Football Association to be competed for by purely amateur clubs, and this club are prepared to offer such a trophy if the Football Association will undertake the management of such a competition.'

Despite an initial decline from the parent body, the FA soon realised their error and, by February 1893, had set the wheels in motion to establish the contest. Ten years later, on April 4, 1904, came the club's greatest triumph…

The road to glory started when they beat Hessle, from near Hull, 5-3 at home, despite going behind and missing a penalty. The visitors played with ten-men for the first half hour as one of their number had missed his train.

In the second round Sheffield won again, this time by 4-1 away to Loughborough Corinthians, and in the third they thrashed Darlington St Augustines 7-0. The semi-finals saw Club cruise comfortably past Bishop Auckland at the Baseball Ground, Derby, by five goals to two in front of a crowd of 1,000 on March 12, 1904.

The stage was set for the final, against Ealing, at Valley Parade, the home of Bradford City, and in the 6,000 crowd Sheffield had plenty of boisterous but good-natured supporters brandishing bells, rattles and horns, all of which helped to create a vibrant atmosphere inside the ground.

According to a local newspaper report, many of the band of enthusiastic Sheffield followers had themselves figured in the team in their earlier days.

A cup winners medal from the 1904 triumph.

Newspaper report of Sheffield FC's Amateur Cup win in 1904. (*Sheffield and Rotherham Independent* 5.4.1904)

Billed as a "keen contest for the blue riband of amateurism", Sheffield were two up at half-time, thanks to goals from J.E. Hoyland after 15 minutes and H. Bedford in the twenty-fifth. A forty-eighth minute penalty by Fred Milnes took the tally to three but the club did not have it all their own way in the second half.

A summary of the game in a local newspaper noted: "In the first half Sheffield Club played much the better game, opening it out well and scoring

Sheffield FC's Amateur Cup winning side of 1904. Players are (in no particular order): Bolsover, Chambers, Milnes, P. Green, Potts, Frost, Sylvester, Bedford, E. Hoyland, G. Hoyland, J.E. Forsdyke. (Photo courtesy of Keith Hardie)

two beautiful goals, the first through a perfect centre by Sylvester which George Hoyland headed on to his brother who burst clean through and got in a wonderful fifteen yards drive which Finlay hardly saw.

"The second was a simpler sort, but equally good, Bedford turning round quickly and beating the goalkeeper with a fast, high shot which completely baffled him. The third goal of the winner's total came from a clearly-deserved penalty whilst, to all appearances, Ealing's one point came through a miskick by one of the Sheffielders after Bolsover had saved.

"Up to the interval it looked any sort of odds on Sheffield; afterwards, had Ealing been able to shoot better, they could hardly have lost. They struggled with the desperation of a dying man and five sixths of this half were fought out in front of the Sheffield goal, where Milnes, Chambers and Bolsover did splendid service.

"As it was they were able to account for the attacks but it cannot be denied, on what was seen in this second half, the Sheffielders were fortunate to carry the trophy North on tour and such magnificent efforts as Ealing put in during the latter stages of the game compelled everyone's admiration."

At the conclusion of the match the cup and mementoes were presented by C.W. Alcock, representing the FA.

As well as alluding to the long

history of Sheffield FC, Alcock also noted that not only had the club "stood by the association and its rules, but they had always upheld the truest principles of amateur football."

Some sources note the absence of Vivian Simpson from Sheffield's ranks during the final. He was, however, also absent from the first round and the semi-final, with another important Sheffield forward, Forsdike, also missing from the latter game.

Simpson had scored a hat-trick in the third round against Darlington. He later went on to play for Sheffield Wednesday and notched another hat-trick, against Manchester United, in an FA Cup tie at Hillsborough.

Sadly, the talented footballer was killed in action in France during the First World War in 1918.

Sheffield FC lined up for the final as follows:

H. Bolsover; F.H. Milnes, F.E.M. Chambers; A.S. Frost, H.A. Potts, W.P. Green; F. Forsdike, J.E. Hoyland, G. Hoyland, H. Bedford, W.S. Sylvester.

After the final-whistle celebrations and presentations, the team dined together at the King's

Brothers Clegg : "Bravo, boys—you make us feel young again".
The glory of old Sheffield Club has been revived by the capture of the Amateur Cup on Monday.

Sheffield FC are presented with the FA Amateur Cup.

Head Hotel in Change Alley – subsequently destroyed by bombing during the Second World War.

The honorary secretary, Mr Willey, was presented with the ball used in the final, photographs of the team, a gold watch and chain, a suitcase, a kit bag and a cricket bag.

The 1903-4 Amateur Cup run

Round 1   Saturday, 23 January 1904   Hessle   H   5-3
G. Hoyland 2, O.G., Potts, Bedford
At Niagara Grounds, Wadsley Bridge   Attendance: Small company
Team: J.A. Turner, J.E. Hoyland, Chambers, Middleton, Sylvester, Greaves, Forsdike, Potts, G. Hoyland, Bedford, G. Turner.

Round 2   Saturday, 13 February 1904   Loughborough Corinthians   A   4-1
Unknown, Simpson, Forsdike, J.E. Hoyland
At Loughborough Athletic Ground   Attendance: 3000

Round 3   Saturday 27 February 1904   Darlington St Augustines   H   7-0
Forsdike, Simpson 3, G. Hoyland 3
At Wadsley Bridge
Team: Bolsover, Potts, Chambers, Middleton, Sylvester, Green, Forsdike, J.E. Hoyland, G. Hoyland, Simpson, Bedford.

Semi-final   Saturday 12 March 1904   Bishop Auckland   5-2
J.E. Hoyland 2, Bedford, G. Hoyland, OG   Attendance: 1000
At Baseball Ground, Derby
Team: Bolsover, Chambers, Milnes, Middleton, Green, Sylvester, Potts, J.E. Hoyland, G. Hoyland, Hibberd, Bedford.

Club Fight Against Professionalism

Sheffield FC has always been an amateur club.

In 1859, following its development by Nathaniel Creswick and William Prest, all playing members had to pay 2s 6d subscription for the year, with payment due on the first day of November.

However, in those early days of the game it was commonplace for players to represent a number of clubs at any one time, depending on fixtures and availability.

AS THE game started to grow, more teams were formed, thereby increasing the competition between clubs to secure the most talented individuals. Professionalism, therefore, seemed inevitable.

However, whenever the issue of players being paid to play football was debated, Sheffield FC was of the opinion that it should be regarded as an "evil to be eliminated once and for all."

Former Sheffield FC player and secretary William F. Beardshaw was one member of the oldest club who was pro-amateurism from the outset. A keen football figure, William also appeared for Sheffield Wednesday, Thursday Wanderers and later became a member of the Football Association.

He progressed to the role of President of the Sheffield Chamber of Commerce and ironically joined the executive committee at Sheffield United – a professional club .

On 31 October 1882 Beardshaw called for the Football Association to set up a sub-committee to look into the payment of players.

He wrote: "It is well known to a large number of followers of Association football that the payment of players gradually crept in by the introduction into Lancashire of proficient exponents of the game from Scotland and elsewhere.

"Unfortunately, the Football Association did not take any steps to stamp out the disease in its infancy and it was not until many English districts suffered from the abstraction of several of their best men that any outcry was made. The (Sheffield) committee were almost unanimously instructed by a general meeting to take steps to suppress what was generally acknowledged as a "Growing Evil.""

Sheffield football legend Charles Clegg was also initially against professionalism.

Clegg, whose long links with the FA were just

beginning, said: "If professionalism is allowed it will only place greater power in the hands of the betting men and if ever the gamblers get control of the game, I wouldn't give tuppence for it."

But over time Sheffield FC officials succumbed to the idea and accepted professionalism, in other clubs at least, as a move forward for the game.

The main drive towards professionalism was ultimately from the Lancashire clubs and many from Sheffield led the resistance to it, despite one player James Lang, coming to the city as probably the first professional in 1876.

James Lang's early clubs in Glasgow included Eastern and Clydesdale, but it was probably whilst playing for Glasgow against a Sheffield representative team in February 1876 and in April of the same year for Clydesdale against Sheffield Wednesday, that he was invited to move to South Yorkshire and play for Wednesday.

Evidence from the 1876-7 season indicates that Lang was resident in Sheffield for virtually the whole of that season. He continued to assist Wednesday throughout this campaign and it is believed the club helped him obtain employment in the city, so that he could play football on Saturdays.

Officials at Sheffield FC had also secured the services of a Nottingham-based England international, Arthur William Cursham, for an FA Cup tie. However, there is no suggestion that Cursham was receiving any monetary reward for his appearance. The practice of representing one team in friendly fixtures whilst choosing an entirely different club for cup ties was perfectly legal at the time.

However, not only were they importing a player from another district, their opponents in the tie were none other than Nottingham FC for whom Cursham had already played regularly in friendly games during that same season.

There were in fact two cup games between the clubs, the first ending in a draw. In an article on the first fixture, a reporter for a Sheffield newspaper noted that Cursham's appearance in the Sheffield XI elicited 'some slight expressions of disapprobation (which were quite improper) from the Nottingham people.'

Despite the practice of players representing multiple clubs being an accepted part of 1870s football, this particular custom was nevertheless much frowned upon in local soccer communities. With some irony, therefore, in December 1877 and February 1878, Cursham lined up for Nottingham against Sheffield in two friendly matches.

There had been 'unofficial' professionalism in football in Britain before it was eventually legalised in 1885. This coincided with a difficult time financially for Sheffield FC, who saw a decline in membership fees with players choosing clubs who paid them.

In 1885, Club had struggled to buy a wooden stand at their Attercliffe ground at a cost of £35. The timber merchant, who was owed most of the money by the club, was offered the return of the timber as part of the re- payment.

The problems continued, with Sheffield FC even playing most of their games out of the city to save costs. Within two years of the legalisation of professionalism, Sheffield FC decided to amalgamate with Collegiate Cricket Club's football team, another high-profile amateur club in the district.

An extraordinary meeting, which Harry Waters Chambers chaired, was called to discuss the matter. It was agreed that two amateur clubs could not exist in the town and it was decided the two should be merged with Sheffield FC retaining their identity.

Club subsequently rejoined the local association and took part in the Challenge Trophy, before going on to see an increase in members and revenue.

Despite those dark days, Sheffield FC's amateurism never wavered and even during the club's centenary year in 1957 they were not allowed to take money from supporters wanting to attend games at their Abbeydale ground. Club had to depend on income from a subscription of a guinea a time.

In 1957 Sheffield FC secretary, Jim Hardie, said: "Our members are just people who want a game on a Saturday, and we try to fit them all in. We estimate some 6,000 players have turned out for us since our formation."

It was a positive indication that from its inception to the current day Sheffield FC has continued its desire of 'playing for the love of the game.'

Sports writer Fred Walters wrote in the Sheffield *Green'Un* newspaper on 19 October 1957: "Professionalism came and has continued to grow, yet do not lose sight of the fact that to keep the 92 Football League clubs going, only a mere 2,000 players are required, whereas up and down England half a million youngsters or more are playing the game week in and week out for the sheer enjoyment of playing.

"Therefore, at a time like this, do not let 92 Football League clubs think they are the be-all and end-all of football. If they all packed up tomorrow, football would go on just the same."

The legalisation of professionalism in 1885 prompted an initial decline in amateur football. Nevertheless, a new development was needed to aid the future of those outside the professional game.

It was the new-look Sheffield FC who headed the initiative by proposing an exciting and innovative competition – the FA Amateur Cup.

Grounds

It is extraordinary to think a football club with such a long and illustrious history could have existed for so long without a place to really call home.

Sheffield FC have had their fair share of grounds, playing at more than ten different sites across the city during their 150-year history – none of which they can truly say was their own.

SOME OF the venues the club has called 'home' include East Bank Road, Ecclesall Road, Olive Grove, Bramall Lane, Niagara grounds, Abbeydale Park, Hillsborough Park, Don Valley Stadium, Woodburn Road and Owlerton Stadium.

However, at the start of 2007 Sheffield FC acquired their first ever ground, purchasing the lease for the land on which their current Bright Finance Stadium now sits.

Never before have they owned the land they played on. Even in the early days, when Sheffield FC was formed in that now infamous greenhouse at Mr Thomas Asline Ward's house in 1857, members played on fields behind the property on East Bank Road.

The lands were taken over by Midland Railway and are now home to a bus depot in the Olive Grove area of Sheffield.

Next came the Newhall Athletic ground in the east of the city and then the Old Forge, both of which have been built on.

In 1862, Sheffield FC were allowed to use Bramall Lane for a one-off game against Hallam in aid of the Lancashire Distress Fund. As we have already mentioned in another section of this book, the game was the first football match at Bramall Lane after the ground's authorities relented to pressure by allowing football to be played on their hallowed cricket surface.

Over the coming years, Bramall Lane itself was acquired for a number of Sheffield FC matches of importance. This became common practice for a number of local clubs, including Sheffield Wednesday.

However, it was never used as a permanent home for Club and there was a good deal of acrimony at times between Sheffield FC and the Bramall Lane authorities, with many bitter disagreements taking place.

This was evident in 1875 when one member of Sheffield FC suggested they should have 'no dealings with Bramall Lane in any circumstances' and even suggested they 'should be told where they could go to.'

Over time the Bramall Lane authorities realised that Association Football was here to stay and

New home help for oldest club

J'ber 14/May 1991

By Jill Ward, Municipal Reporter

SHEFFIELD FC — the oldest soccer club in the world — have been thrown a lifelife by the City Council to help them reclaim a place in the top regional league.

And it could see them playing at the showpiece Don Valley Stadium.

In 1989 the club were automatically relegated from the Weekly Wynner League Premier Division after their ground at Hillsborough Park arena was judged by officials not to be up to league standard.

The club had to play in Division One after a financial deal with Sheffield Council and the Football Association to upgrade the ground fell through.

Now recreation chiefs are recommending the club is allowed to use, either free or for a token fee, the showpiece Don Valley Stadium for next season's early matches until their new home at Woodbourn Road athletics stadium is ready later this year.

"It is projected that October will see Woodbourn Road operational, and rather than have Sheffield Football Club waiting another year for promotion, it is suggested the first team allowed to play their first few home matches at the nearby Don Valley Stadium," says a council report.

But recreation chiefs fear the estimated £250 fee for using the stadium by Sheffield FC would pose a serious financial difficulty for the club and instead are recommending it be charged either a part or none of the club has invested in the Hillsborough Park arena which is owned by the council.

A newspaper clipping of Sheffield FC moving to Don Valley Stadium. (*Sheffield Star* 14 May 1991)

agreed for more teams to use their stadium for key games.

During the early part of the 20th Century, Sheffield FC were playing their home matches at the Niagara Grounds in Wadsley Bridge, now just a stone's throw away from Sheffield Wednesday's Hillsborough Stadium.

In 1911 Sheffield FC along with the Collegiate Cricket Club and Sheffield Rugby Union Football Club were invited to join Sheffield Hockey Club in a combined use of the pitches at the Richmond Ground in Handsworth.

Within a year all three agreed and the Sheffield Amateur Sports Club was established to become the only club of its kind in the United Kingdom.

However, the outbreak of the First World War in 1914 brought a halt to amateur sport in Sheffield with the Richmond ground's clubs losing their venue. After the war the Amateur Sports Club decided to look for an alternative home and in 1919 the Handsworth site was sold to purchase the playing fields at Abbeydale Park.

The site was bought at an auction for £4,500 and, by September 1921, it had officially became the new home of Sheffield Amateur Sports Club, which of course included Sheffield FC.

Abbeydale Park. A former Sheffield FC ground for more than 60 years. (FA news publication)

Club went on to spend more than 60 years at Abbeydale Park, which still remains one of the fondest venues in their history and possibly the only ground before the present one that came close to truly being called home.

It proved a successful place for Club, with the venue enjoying excellent facilities and commuting links for members, players and spectators. Sheffield FC also achieved success on the field at Abbeydale, winning promotion to the First Division of the Yorkshire League during the 1954-55 season.

A sign of how good the facilities were at Abbeydale Park was confirmed when the national sides of Argentina and Switzerland used Sheffield FC's ground for training during the 1966 World Cup in England.

In the summer of 1988 Sheffield FC had to leave their home at Abbeydale Park because the dressing rooms were deemed by the league too far away from the pitch.

Club opted to play at Hillsborough Park. The return to the 'Sheffield 6' area of the city did not prove to be a successful switch. A year later, Club were relegated from the Weekly Wynner League Premier Division after league officials decided that the Hillsborough Park ground was not up to league standards.

The club were forced to play in Division One after a deal with the Football Association and Sheffield City Council to upgrade the Hillsborough venue fell through.

Discussions with the Council continued and soon after Sheffield FC secured a move to the newly built Don Valley Stadium. The modern 25,000-seater venue was and still is one of the largest sporting venues in the city and a world away from the club's previous ground.

Switching venues to Don Valley Stadium coincided with a difficult time for the club financially. Sheffield FC struggled to attract any real support at games, especially as both Wednesday and United were enjoying success in the newly-formed Premier League.

It was agreed that a move to a smaller venue

would be more appropriate and Sheffield FC changed 'home' once more by moving to Owlerton Stadium.

However, the switch was temporary as Club had real ambitions to secure a ground of their own to help their financial situation and safeguard the club's future.

Peter Beeby was chairman when in 2001, Sheffield FC moved to Dronfield on the outskirts of the city to play next to the Coach and Horses public house on Sheffield Road. On 21 April 2001 the club played its first Northern Counties Eastern League Premier Division game at their new home against Thackley.

However, the ground was officially unveiled three months later when Manchester United sent a representative side to play against Sheffield FC – a pennant from the game can still be seen behind the bar at the Coach and Horses!

It was a sign of future times as the club began to use its position as the oldest in the world by attracting interest from the world's top clubs.

Lord Pendry, chairman of the Football Foundation and then Sports Minister Richard Caborn MP also attended the official opening ceremony.

Three years later a unique sponsorship deal with Chapeltown-based company Bright Finance was agreed for the stadium, which has become known as the Bright Finance Stadium and affectionately as the Stadium of Bright.

Former Sheffield Wednesday and Crystal Palace striker Mark Bright

A Sheffield FC game at their home ground of Abbeydale Park.

Former Sheffield Wednesday striker Mark Bright and Bright Finance Chairman Paul Hancock at the Bright Finance Stadium.

joined Bright Finance chairman and Sheffield FC director Paul Hancock and Club chairman Richard Tims to officially announce the renaming of the stadium.

At the launch, TV presenter and football pundit Bright said: "It's nice to be involved in the launch – not many people can say their name is linked to a football stadium!

"I was aware that Sheffield FC were the oldest football club in the world, following my time with Wednesday, but I wasn't sure where they played. I think it's fantastic that the club is still going and preserving a piece of history in the game. It's great to think that football started right here."

Ahead of the 150th anniversary, the club purchased the lease for their stadium in a ground-breaking six-figure deal, following financial investment from the newly formed board of directors. The Sheffield FC board includes Paul Hancock, Jim Harrison, Mark Goodband and Simon Webster, along with chairman Richard Tims.

As part of the purchase, Club also took over the running of the Coach and Horses public house which provides extra revenue for the amateur side. It was a major feat and a unique moment in their history as Sheffield FC formally enjoyed their first official ground in 150 years.

Centenary
Celebrations

Sheffield FC's remarkable achievement of becoming the first football club in the world to reach 100 years was marked with a number of centenary celebration events in October, 1957.

THE IMPORTANCE of the anniversary was evident when a committee which included key officials from Club, the Sheffield FA, Sheffield Wednesday and Sheffield United was established three years in advance of the occasion!

During centenary year, Sheffield FC had three teams in three different leagues – the Yorkshire League, the Sheffield Association League and the South Yorkshire Amateur League – and more than 40 players on its books.

Club secretary Jim Hardie, who had also played for Sheffield FC as a forward from 1939 until 1947, was a leading figure behind the anniversary celebrations.

He told the *Sheffield Star* at the time: "After all, we're 100 years old this year and we don't mean to let the event pass unnoticed."

A 72-page centenary booklet produced by Fred Walters, then sports editor of the *Sheffield Star* and *Green 'Un*, was published to mark Sheffield FC's

All-star teams miss chance to boost amateurs

By DAVE PARDON

Selected Amateur XI ...... 2 Queen's Park 2

BRAMALL LANE on its best behaviour is quite something; no boos, raucous cries of "above it" or suggestions that the referee visit an optician. Instead, polite handclaps for the good moves, sympathetic "tut-tuts" for the failings.

In fact there was an unusual — definitely amateur — atmosphere about the place yesterday. But then it was an unusual occasion—no other soccer club in the world has yet been able to celebrate — as Sheffield Football Club did yesterday—100 years of soccer life.

It was a great day for Sheffield soccer, and the organisers had spared no pains to do the game, the club, and the city, proud.

For the players—pick of Britain's unpaid performers—it was the chance of a lifetime to boost amateur soccer in a professional-minded city.

An excuse

Regrettably the chance was missed. As an exhibition match it fell below expectations, as a counter-attraction to the professional game it just wasn't.

For the Selected XI, assembled the night before with just time for a brief tactical chat from team-manager Joe Mercer, there was, perhaps, an excuse. But Queen's Park are a Scottish League first division side and I, for one, hoped for much better than we saw.

The neat short-passing on-the-ground game normally associated with the Scots was missing. In its place was a deal of aimless kicking, lofted passes and, after one 25-yard volley by Brown in the first half, able to beat the best out of Pegasus and England goalkeeper Mike Pinner.

Best moves of the match came in fact from the scratch eleven. And of that side I take top marks to centre-half Corbett Cresswell, winging some honours to the right wing pair of Barnsley's Frank Bean mont and Sheffield United's Bills

AMERICANS TOP CANADA CUP LIST

TOKYO, Thursday

AMERICA'S Sam Snead and Jimmy Demaret, defending title practice-home, took a commanding lead in the first round of the Canada Cup tournament.

The 6,000-yard par-72 Japan woodland golf course the pace with a 143. Snead and Demaret were two strokes better than third-placed Australia and close behind were Argentina and Wales.

Only three players beat 70 — Snead (65), Demaret (69), Torakichi Nakamura (68), and only two others beat the high-scoring Country Club course's par 72. Jumbo Nason

ONLY STEADY

English Ryder Cup players Peter Alliss and Ken Bousfield steady

SHEFFIELD FOOTBALL CLUB
CENTENARY

SHEFFIELD

versus

ENGLAND 'B'

WEDNESDAY, 23rd OCTOBER, 1957

Kick-off 7.15 p.m.

(BY FLOODLIGHT)

Hillsborough

A match programme from a game between Sheffield and an England B side staged at Hillsborough to mark 100 years of the club.

Sheffield FC 1950 team. Sheffield FC line-up for game with Norton Woodseats on Christmas Day 1950. The photo is believed to be taken at the club's current stadium in Dronfield. Front row (from left to right): Bill Benson, Alan Smith, Tommy Graton, Keith Smith and Pete Copley (who supplied photo). Back row (from left to right): Harry Parkin (c), Alan Pashley, Harold Marsden, Bill Skinner, unknown, Bob Nesbitt and Frank Fagan (trainer).

anniversary. It charted a brief history of the club from 1857 to 1957 and included a foreword from Arthur Drewry, President of FIFA and Chairman of the Football Association.

Drewry's words, and his attendance at the club's 100th celebration banquet on October 24, were in triumphant recognition of Sheffield FC's unique position in the game and a testament to the organisers of the anniversary.

The first event in a week of celebrations was a concert at the Empire Theatre, Sheffield on 20 October, with skiffle king Lonnie Donegan the headline act.

The Duke of Edinburgh attends the annual dinner to mark 100 years of Sheffield FC. (*Sheffield Newspapers*). Sir Stanley Rous, President of the FA, Dr. C. O. Greer, President of Sheffield FC, H.R.H The Duke of Edinburgh, Sir Frederick Pickworth (Master Cutler), The Earl of Scarborough, Ald. A. Ballard (Lord Mayor of Sheffield).

A team photo of Sheffield FC from 1955. (*Sheffield Newspapers*).
Back row (from left to right): Trusswell, Cann, Gleadall, Palfreyman, Pashley, Lane, Burn, Fagan and Wheatley. Front row (from left to right): Grainger, Wragg, Smith, Robinson, Havenhead, Wasden and Shelton.

Also on the bill was singer and former Sheffield United player Colin Grainger, local group the Savoy Quintet, recording artist Cynthia Lannigan and Russ Hamilton. Sheffield FC President, Dr Charles Greer was another key member of the centenary committee and he commented in his programme notes at the concert: "The popularity of this show and the wise choice of artists was shown by the immediate rush for seats.

"I would like to record my particular appreciation of Mr Donegan's response. When some time ago he was asked to appear, I am told that without any hesitation he agreed to appear, although the only beneficiaries would obviously be yourselves and Sheffield Club."

One of the best attended and most prestigious events during the centenary week was an international clash between a Sheffield XI and an England 'B' side at Hillsborough on 23 October 1957.

The England 'B' team included a number of the country's best players, all of whom were on the fringes of the national first-team. One of these was Manchester United's young star Eddie Colman, who just four months later was killed in the Munich air disaster.

Also in the side was Ronnie Allen, a player tipped for England honours and West Brom team-mate Bobby Robson, who went on to lead England to the World Cup semi-finals more than 30 years later.

SS' EMPIRE THEATRE — SHEFFIELD

EMPIRE THEATRE — SHEFFIELD

Managing Director: VAL PARNELL

Manager: JOHN SPITZER
Assistant Manager: EDWIN SHAW

an: PRINCE LITTLER
Manager: ERNEST FENTON

★ **THE LONNIE DONEGAN SHOW** ★

PROGRAMME

Compered by PETER QUINTON

Musical Director: MAURICE NEWTON

INTERVAL

The Lord Mayor of Sheffield
(Alderman Albert Ballard, C.B.E., J.P.)
OFFICIALLY OPENS THE CENTENARY WEEK
and introduces . . .

★

THE SAVOY QUINTET

LONNIE DONEGAN

★

★

...IN GRAINGER

KEN TURNER & HIS MI...

CYNTHIA LANN'...

RUSS HAM...
with DEREK NEW...

The Managem...

SHEFFIELD FOOTBALL CLUB

1857
S.F.C.
1957
Billin

CENTENARY

CONCERT

PRESENTED BY

LONNIE DONEGAN

EMPIRE THEATRE, SHEFFIELD
SUNDAY, 20th OCTOBER, 1957

SOUVENIR PROGRAMME — ONE SHILLING

entenary Concert – centre. A centre-spread
nd front page from the programme at the
entenary concert which featured Lonnie
onegan.

Jim Hardie. Former Sheffield FC secretary during the 100th anniversary.

Centenary Committee. The centenary committee which was established to mark Sheffield FCs 100th anniversary.
Front row (left to right): W. S. Crookes, J. Hardie, Dr. C. O. Greer, M. Wheatley, F. Allan. Back row: Fred Walters, Eric Taylor (Secretary-manager Sheffield Wednesday), John Spitzer, Ernest Kangley (Secretary Sheffield and Hallamshire FA). Arnold Newton (secretary Sheffield United) was also a member of the committee but was not present for the photo.

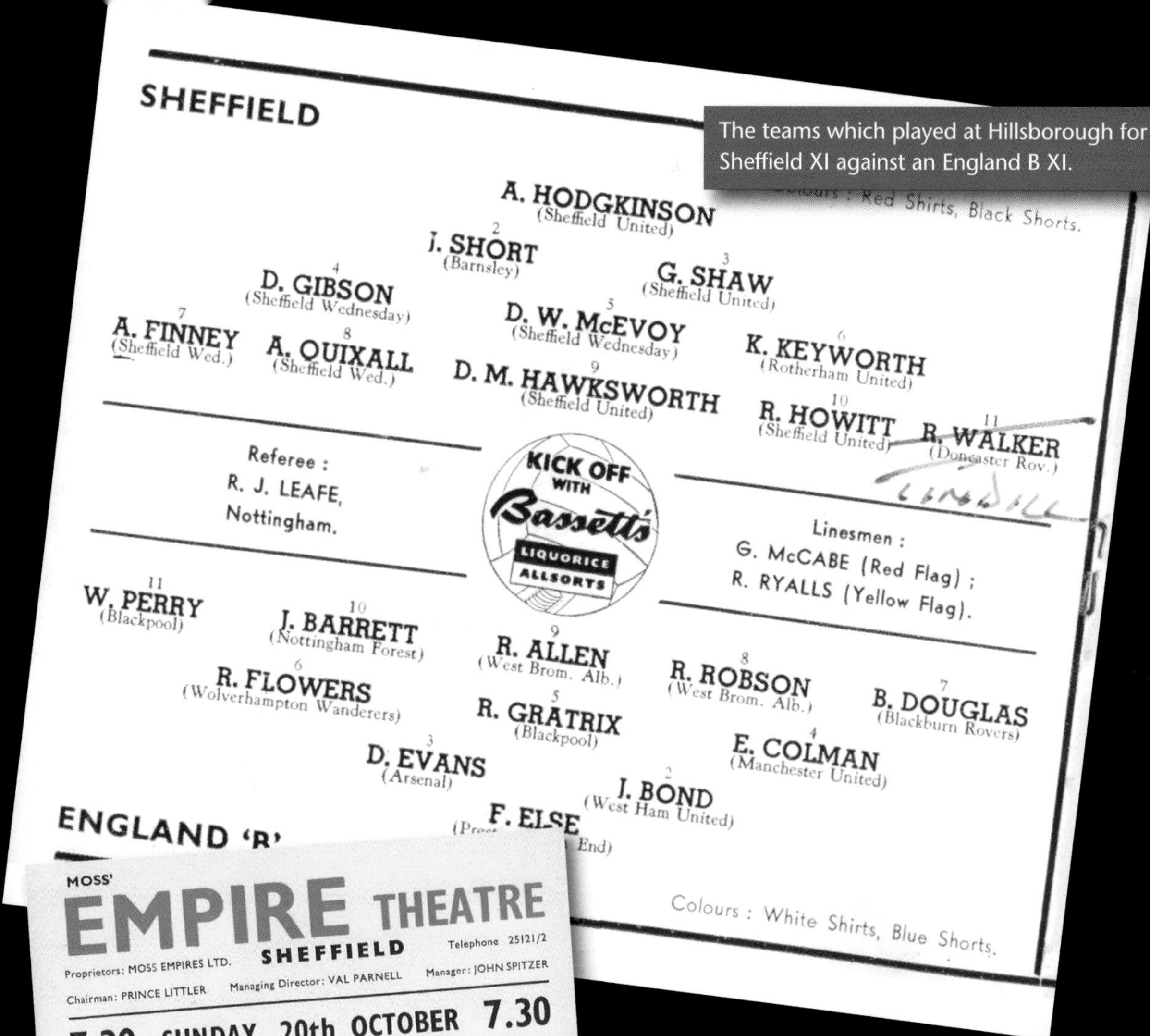

The teams which played at Hillsborough for a Sheffield XI against an England B XI.

SHEFFIELD

A. HODGKINSON
(Sheffield United)

J. SHORT
(Barnsley)

G. SHAW
(Sheffield United)

D. GIBSON
(Sheffield Wednesday)

D. W. McEVOY
(Sheffield Wednesday)

K. KEYWORTH
(Rotherham United)

A. FINNEY
(Sheffield Wed.)

A. QUIXALL
(Sheffield Wed.)

D. M. HAWKSWORTH
(Sheffield United)

R. HOWITT
(Sheffield United)

R. WALKER
(Doncaster Rov.)

Referee :
R. J. LEAFE,
Nottingham.

KICK OFF
WITH
Bassett's
LIQUORICE
ALLSORTS

Linesmen :
G. McCABE (Red Flag) ;
R. RYALLS (Yellow Flag).

W. PERRY
(Blackpool)

J. BARRETT
(Nottingham Forest)

R. ALLEN
(West Brom. Alb.)

R. ROBSON
(West Brom. Alb.)

B. DOUGLAS
(Blackburn Rovers)

R. FLOWERS
(Wolverhampton Wanderers)

R. GRATRIX
(Blackpool)

E. COLMAN
(Manchester United)

D. EVANS
(Arsenal)

J. BOND
(West Ham United)

F. ELSE
(Preston... End)

ENGLAND 'B'

Colours : White Shirts, Blue Shorts.

Centenary concert – poster – A poster from the centenary concert which featured Lonnie Donegan.

The side was:

Fred Else (Preston North End), John Bond (West Ham United), Dennis Evans (Arsenal), Eddie Colman (Manchester United), Roy Gratrix (Blackpool), Ron Flowers (Wolves), Bryan Douglas (Blackburn Rovers), Bobby Robson (West Bromwich Albion), Ronnie Allen (West Bromwich Albion), Jim Barrett (Nottingham Forest) and Bill Perry (Blackpool)

The Sheffield XI, a representative side of South Yorkshire-based players, was akin to those early Sheffield teams in the game's beginning during the 1870s.

The full XI was:

Alan Hodgkinson (Sheffield United), John Short (Barnsley), Graham Shaw (Sheffield United), Don Gibson (Sheffield Wednesday), Don McEvoy captain (Sheffield Wednesday), Ken Keyworth (Rotherham United), Alan Finney (Sheffield Wednesday), Albert Quix-all (Sheffield Wednesday), Derek Hawks-worth (Sheffield United), Bobby Howitt (Sheffield United) and Bert Tindill (Don-caster Rovers).

Before the game, a message in the match programme from Sheffield Wednesday read: "It is not inappropriate that the Sheffield Wednesday club should stage this fixture, for although our club was not formed until ten years after Sheffield Club, many players have often played for both teams. We will name only a few, such as the late Sir Charles and Sir William Clegg, Herbert Newbould, T.E.B. Wilson and Daff Davy.

"We think the whole soccer world should be made aware of the important contribution Sheffield Club has made to the game and realise that this first centenary in football is infinitely more than just another anniversary.

"Sheffield Club are to be heartily congratulated on their great achievement and on so worthily maintaining through the century the best and highest principles of the game and good sportsmanship."

A crowd of 25,000 turned up at Hillsborough to enjoy the spectacle, which ended in a 5-4 win for the national team, despite a late disallowed goal from the local side.

The score had been 2-1 to the Sheffield XI after just six minutes. Bobby Robson began the goal spree with an early strike for the national side, only for Sheffield Wednesday's Albert Quixall, who a few seasons before had been in the England team, to equalise. Quixall then set up Sheffield United's Derek Hawksworth to give Sheffield the lead.

Ronnie Allen levelled the scores on 24 minutes, before the West Brom forward grabbed another with a shot which was deflected in off Don McEvoy to put England 3-2 up. Sheffield were again level three minutes later when Bobby Howitt dummied his way past two defenders and fired the ball past the keeper.

Hawksworth added a fourth just before half-time to give Sheffield the lead. However, in the second-half two goals from Robson secured his hat-trick and the win for England.

A day later it was Bramall Lane's turn to host an English amateur XI against Queen's Park – the oldest club in Scotland. Queen's Park, formed in 1867, has kept its amateur status throughout its existence, just like Sheffield FC.

When invited to send its first team to play in the centenary celebrations, Queen's Park secretary James Logan, replied: "We shall be delighted to do so. We have put the suggestion before our players and they were readily agreeable. We consider it a great honour to be asked to take part in the occasion."

The game was another fascinating contest with the score ending in a 2-2 draw, with more than 5,000 in attendance, including His Royal Highness the Duke of Edinburgh.

Geoff Robinson, Sheffield FC's only player in the game, scored an 80th minute equaliser for the representative side, managed by Joe Mercer.

Jimmy Devine had given Queen's Park the lead before Accrington Stanley's Mike Tracey equalised. Malcolm Garroch then put the team from north of the border back in front, before Robinson levelled.

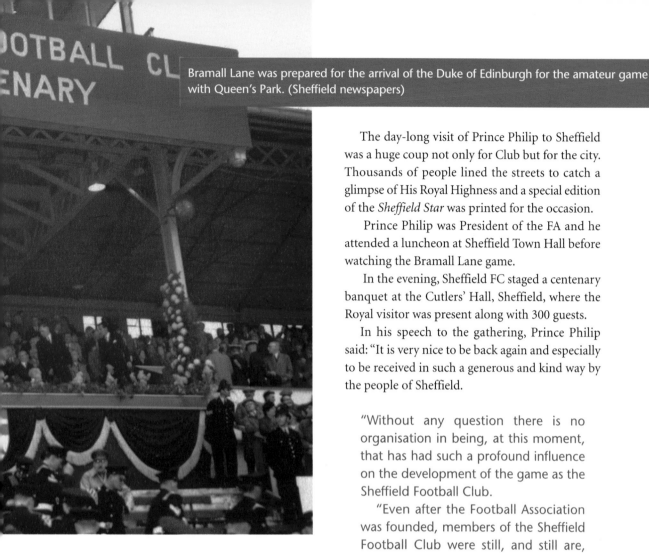

The day-long visit of Prince Philip to Sheffield was a huge coup not only for Club but for the city. Thousands of people lined the streets to catch a glimpse of His Royal Highness and a special edition of the *Sheffield Star* was printed for the occasion.

Prince Philip was President of the FA and he attended a luncheon at Sheffield Town Hall before watching the Bramall Lane game.

In the evening, Sheffield FC staged a centenary banquet at the Cutlers' Hall, Sheffield, where the Royal visitor was present along with 300 guests.

In his speech to the gathering, Prince Philip said: "It is very nice to be back again and especially to be received in such a generous and kind way by the people of Sheffield.

"Without any question there is no organisation in being, at this moment, that has had such a profound influence on the development of the game as the Sheffield Football Club.

"Even after the Football Association was founded, members of the Sheffield Football Club were still, and still are, listened to with respect. I'm not surprised because it would take an ingenious mind, and I suspect a Yorkshire mind, to think of putting their players in kid gloves and clutching half crowns to stop them handling the ball!"

Here, the Prince was referring to a system used by Sheffield FC players during the early days of the club's history to deter them from using their hands. (Please see 'Sheffield – home of football' chapter for more details).

His Royal Highness continued, saying:

"Sheffield Club really started something 100 years ago because there is no doubt that

The full teams were:

Amateur XI: M. J. Pinner (Pegasus), B. Smith (Manchester United), D. J. Wright (Barnsley), D. Barber (Barnsley), C. Cresswell (Bishop Auckland), S. O'Connell (Middlesbrough), A. Beaumont (Barnsley), W. Russell (Sheffield United), G. N. Robinson (Sheffield FC), M. G. Tracey (Accrington Stanley), K. Fountain (Harrogate Railway Athletic).

Queen's Park: F. Crampsey, I.G. Harnett, W. M. Hastie, R.L. Cromar, J. F. Robb, J. Chalmers, E. B. Brown, W. L. Black, A. P. McEwan, J. H. Devine, C. Church.

The Duke of Edinburgh meets Joe Mercer, manager of the Amateur XI chosen to play against Queen's Park at Bramall Lane. (Sheffield newspapers)

The Duke of Edinburgh sits among Sheffield FC officials and guests at the Centenary banquet at the Cutlers' Hall. (Sheffield Newspapers).

ALLEN GRABS GOALS—AND THE GLORY

Sheffield XI 4,
England B 5

By
ARCHIE LEDBROOKE

THIS match was put on as part of the Sheffield Soccer centenary celebrations — it turned out to be a West Bromwich beano!

Ronnie Allen (2) and Bobby Robson (3) scored all the England goals.

Better still, they gave an exhibition of Hungarian-style football that turned a friendly game into a classic demonstration.

Allen is the recognised "king-maker" of the football world. He made Johnny Nicholls into an international and he has helped Derek Kevan to win caps.

So Alert

Under the Sheffield lights he helped Bobby Robson to a hat-trick—and played the Revie plan better than Revie himself!

No one in the game can find a vacant patch of grass away from opponents like this alert little man.

He finds a parking place for himself like a caravan owner at the end of a long day's run. He must be in line for a World Cup place on this show—

good, rarely catches a selector's eye.

The rush of goals de-lighted the fans. England started it in three minutes and along came the shots with never more than one goal between the sides.

Brilliant Else

Sheffield, with players from Wednesday, United, Barnsley, Doncaster and Rotherham, were in front at 2—1 and 4—3 then fell behind again and in a stirring rally could not beat the brilliant goalkeeping of Preston's Fred Else.

One man who couldn't get among the goals was Jim Barrett of Nottingham Forest, but he performed something approaching the impossible.

He headed against the bar, let fly with his foot at the rebound and hit the post. That was his lot for the night.

Sheffield scorers were Oxall, Hawksworth

It looks a certain goal from Jim Barrett, the England "B" inside forward. But that was not counting on Sheffield goalkeeper, Hodgkinson. He saved this one.

A Daily Mirror match report on the centenary game between an England B side and a Sheffield representative XI.

The Duke of Edinburgh meets a Queen's Park player at the centenary game at Bramall Lane.

CENTENARY CELEBRATION MATCH

1857 - 1957

SHEFFIELD FOOTBALL CLUB

versus

QUEEN'S PARK

BRAMALL LANE GROUND, SHEFFIELD

THURSDAY, 24th OCTOBER, 1957
Kick-off 2.45 p.m.

A match programme for the game between a Sheffield FC amateur XI side and Queen's Park.

the game is the most popular game in the United Kingdom today, and in fact it is played all over the world.

"I maintain that it is more fun to play football than it is to watch. The fact that so many millions watch football every week is, to my mind, less important than the vigour and health of amateur clubs, such as the Sheffield Football Club and Queen's Park.

"The amateur clubs are the back-bone of the game in this country. And I would also like to add that the voluntary work which people give in their spare time in running the amateur clubs, they,

in my opinion, are the back-bone of the amateur clubs. Football as a whole owes them a great deal and I hope devoted people like them will continue to come forward.

"I wish all prosperity and every success to the Sheffield Football Club in the next 100 years."

The Duke was presented with a tankard and a piece of cutlery by Sheffield FC's Tommy Brooksbank, who joked with Prince Philip that he would expect the traditional exchange of the proverbial coin in return. As the player was returning to his

seat, Prince Philip called him back, reached into his pocket and handed over a coin.

During the dinner, Sheffield FC President Dr Charles Greer, who had also played for Club, was duly awarded with a testimonial by the Prince on behalf of the FA for his services to football.

Dr Greer responded by saying: "Tonight we proudly celebrate the culmination of our centenary events.

"Although our voice in the football world is not so powerful as of yore, and though our playing strength may not measure up to what it may have done in the past, we don't mind that at all. Because we play football as it was always intended to be played. We play it for pleasure.

"We take particular pride that our predecessors were so largely responsible for what is now a major world sport."

Arthur Drewry, President of FIFA and Chairman of the Football Association, and Sir Stanley Rous, Secretary of the Football Association, were both at the banquet. It was a great honour for Sheffield FC to have present such high profile figures from the world of football at the time.

Sir Stanley Rous told the *Sheffield Star* on 24 October 1957: "The centenary of Sheffield Club is not just another anniversary, nor is it one of interest only to local supporters or those with an extra long memory.

"Properly seen, it is an event which should command attention throughout the country and I would go even further to state that it deserves the interest of the soccer fraternity throughout the whole of the world."

Also at the dinner were the Presidents of the Scottish FA, the Football League, the Yorkshire League and representatives from Queen's Park Football Club, Sheffield Wednesday, Sheffield United, Hallam, Norton and amateur side Pegasus.

Along with a number of former Sheffield FC players, three members of Club's 1904 Amateur Cup winning side were in attendance, Fred Forsdyke, Percy Green and Col. Middleton.

Club on Tour

Sheffield FC quickly recognised that interest in football was spreading, not only beyond the surrounding area of the city but even throughout the world.

IN THE early days of the club's long and illustrious history, Sheffield FC were keen to spread the word of where football originated. The city's involvement with games in Scotland has already been mentioned, but Club also enjoyed a number of tours into Europe and even further afield.

In April 1894 Sheffield FC embarked on their first trip to play in the Netherlands and then to Belgium the following year. There is even a claim that Sheffield FC was 'the first team onto the continent'.

How true this statement is would be difficult to prove, but English textiles workers are believed to have taken football to the Netherlands around the 1860s and by 1889 the country had a Football Association. The same year an FA was established in Denmark, where the oldest club, KB, had been started by a group of Englishmen in 1878.

Sheffield FC's strong links with the Netherlands continued when they travelled into Europe to play a friendly against FC Eindhoven in June 1946. The Sheffield squad involved players from Club, Norton Woodseats and a handful of professionals from the city. Sheffield won 3-0 against Eindhoven and a trophy from the encounter is still in the hands of the oldest club.

At the time, Eindhoven were bigger than their city rivals PSV Eindhoven and the club was the last Dutch league champions before the introduction of professionalism in the Netherlands in 1954.

The games between the two cities were arranged through the Sheffield-Eindhoven branch of the Anglo-Dutch Sports Association – formed to develop relations between the two countries through sport – and the Sheffield and Hallamshire County FA.

Former England and Sheffield Wednesday player Billy Marsden had also been a coach in Holland before the war.

Two months later, FC Eindhoven visited Sheffield, playing at Hillsborough and Bramall Lane, winning both games 1-0 and 2-0 respectively. This time the Sheffield side also included players from Sheffield Wednesday and Sheffield United. Around 14,000 people attended the game at Bramall Lane.

The programme notes for the games in Sheffield read: "A hearty welcome is accorded to the visitors from Eindhoven. We hope they are enjoying their stay and that the trip will be the foundation of lasting friendship between the two cities.

"We ask you to give the Eindhoven party a good reception. Most of them were kind to British

A Sheffield FC team from Easter 1890 during a five-game tournament in which they won three and drew two. Back row – G.H. Aizlewood, T.B.A. Clarke, B.L. Shaw, R.W. Clarke, F.H. Colley (Umpire). Middle row – A.E. Bingham, T. Jowett, E.C. Benson, W.F. Beardshaw (captain), W.T. Wright, G.A. Parker, W. Robinson. Front row – H.B. Willey (Hon. Sec), G.J. Groves, S.C. Hickson.

Servicemen during the war and many were underground fighters against the Germans."

Sheffield FC returned to the Netherlands in 1947, between 14-20 June, with FC Eindhoven once more the hosts. This time a tournament had been devised as Club played in a round-robin style event against Eindhoven, NAC (later to be NAC Breda) and PSV. Sheffield beat Eindhoven 1-0, but lost 2-0 to NAC.

During the trip a Club side took on an RAF XI in Eindhoven as links between Sheffield and the Dutch city continued.

In our initial research to discover how the link between Sheffield and Eindhoven came about a heart-warming tale was uncovered. Stories had emanated from Sheffield how soldiers from the city, some of whom were players of Club, had been involved in the liberation of Eindhoven during the Second World War.

A promise had been made by the soldiers to

group of Sheffield FC players was discovered in two scrapbooks belonging to Mrs Elizabeth Steels of North Wheatley near Retford, in Nottinghamshire.

They had been assiduously compiled by her father Waring Stanser, a prominent amateur player who turned out for Rotherham Town and Sheffield FC. Stanser was a half-back and described as a clever and very effective player who was selected for the North against the South in an amateur international trial at Tottenham Hotspur's White Hart Lane ground.

His books catalogued a 1909 tour of the United States by an amateur representative team called the Pilgrims.

Football in America had begun 40 years earlier with the first organised game of football taking place between Princeton and Rutgers Universities on 6 November 1869. Other pro-kicking colleges later joined the fold, giving 'soccer' a tenuous foothold in this area of American life.

However, following extensive persuasion from Harvard University, the game lost ground to a more rugby form, which later became known as American football. It also lagged behind baseball, which had at that time become a professional sport in the U.S.

The Pilgrims had toured the U.S and Canada four years before, in 1905. Frederick Houghton Milnes, a talented and well-known Sheffield amateur player, was involved in that first tour. Milnes was born in Wortley on 26 January 1878 and was described in one Canadian newspaper as being an iron founder at Owlerton, near Sheffield.

He played for a number of clubs including Sheffield Wycliffe, Sheffield FC, Sheffield United, West Ham United, Tottenham Hotspur, Manchester United, Leicester City, Reading, Ilford and Norwich City.

Milnes was part of the Sheffield FC team which won the FA Amateur Cup in 1904 and subsequently was the moving spirit behind the Pilgrims.

It was reported that the Pilgrims were specially

return with Sheffield FC after the war to play in a friendly competition against the local clubs.

Club also had successful tours to Belgium in 1959 and 1960, being unbeaten in both tours and winning the Burgomasters Cup in Brussels.

Sheffield FC were again invited to play in Eindhoven in June 1962 to mark the 40th anniversary of RKVV Brabantia. Club played against three Eindhoven teams De Spechten, Tongelre and Brabantia during the two-day event. De Spechten, a rather successful club at the time, ceased to exist in the early 1990s.

One of the most interesting tours involving a

A Sheffield FC team which travelled to Eindhoven in 1962 to play in a tournament for the 40th anniversary of RKVV Brabantia.

Winston Barker. President of Soccer Football Association in America and promoter of the Pilgrims tour.

the side moved south into the United States, to St. Louis and Boston.

Before returning to England, captain Milnes and forward Vivian Woodward were invited for a personal meeting with President Roosevelt at the White House, to discuss the sport of soccer.

This initial tour was regarded as a success and in 1909 Milnes was invited to take another team to the US by the American International Soccer Football Association. Milnes, now captain and organiser of the Pilgrims, was joined by two other Sheffield Club players C. Coopland and Stanser.

Coopland, an inside left forward who also enjoyed spells with Hillsborough Board School, Sheffield Wednesday and Glossop, had been to America with Milnes in 1905. He was noted as playing a 'very stylish game' and an effective player who 'shoots terribly hard.' He was a schoolmaster in Sheffield.

The team also included players from Woolwich Arsenal, Darlington, Fulham, Queen's Park and Falkirk.

The announcement of the departure of the tour party appeared in the *Sheffield Daily Telegraph* on Monday, 27 September 1909:

AMATEURS LEAVE FOR AMERICA

On Saturday the Pilgrims, a team of English amateurs footballers, left Liverpool for a tour through the United States and Canada. Four years ago a Pilgrim combination visited the United States and their second trip is the result of their remarkable success, which attended the efforts of the Pilgrims on their last visit, when they accomplished so much in popularising the game in a land where baseball holds sway. It is a sign of the American times that a second invitation was sent to Mr F.H. Milnes, the well-known Sheffield amateur, to bring out a team. He has succeeded in obtaining the services of

selected by US President Theodore Roosevelt, who was conducting a campaign to eliminate brutality from American college football by increasing the popularity of soccer.

Milnes mentioned in his reports back to England that two deaths had taken place as a result of injuries in college football in the US. This made American football increasingly unpopular and added to soccer's appeal.

Although the famous Corinthians club visited the United States in 1906, 1907 and 1911, the Pilgrims tour of 1905 represents the first serious attempt to popularise association football in that country.

All the players were selected from the leading English amateur clubs of the day and Sheffield FC's success in the Amateur Cup had placed the club in the spotlight as one of the best exponents of the sport.

The Pilgrims' first visit started in Canada before

SIZING UP THE PUNT.

PILGRIM TEAM DRIBBLING THE BALL DOWN THE FIELD.

Pictures from Pilgrims first game in New York, October 1904.

A team photo of the Pilgrims team to tour the United States.

fifteen players in all. Nine of them are amateur internationals.

Highlighting the games ahead for the Pilgrims, the report added:

"At Baltimore the players will have the novel experience of playing a match at midnight by the aid of electric light. This match is expected to attract an enormous attendance, for quite recently 17,000 spectators watched an inter-college match under similar conditions. The Pilgrims will also meet a selected team of American players for the possession of the Cochrane Cup presented by Sir Ernest C Cochrane on the occasion of the last visit."

The team travelled from Liverpool to New York on the Mauretania, which on that journey captured the Blue Riband for the fastest westbound crossing of the Atlantic – a record that was to stand for more than 20 years.

The ship took four days, ten hours and 51 minutes, knocking 44 minutes off the previous record.

On the outbreak of the First World War, the *Mauretania* and her sister ship *Lusitania* were wanted by the British government for use as armed merchant cruisers, but their huge size and massive fuel consumption made them unsuitable for the duty and they resumed civilian service. Later, because of a lack of passengers crossing the Atlantic during the war, *Mauretania* was laid up in Liverpool until May 1915, and the *Lusitania*, which the players had used for their return trip to England, was later sunk by a German U-boat.

On arrival at the east coast of America, Milnes underlined the team's mission in an interview with the *New York Times*, saying: "We came to America to demonstrate Association Football as it is played in England. We heard that the game was not generally played in the United States.

"Our idea was to come over and start a boom for it, which would result in popularising it and

THE PILGRIMS' TOUR.

SECOND TRIP TO THE STATES.

Last night the members of the Pilgrims' football touring party, who sail from Liverpool, to-day, on the Mauretania, at five o'clock, dined together at the North-Western Hotel, Liverpool. The most complete arrangements have been made for the journey. The players are accommodated in five rooms on board, the three Sheffield members of the party, whose portraits we give below, being in Room 5 E.

The programme is a very extensive one, commencing with a match against All New York, at Staten Island, on 2 October. Further fixtures are against Sons of St. George, at Baltimore; Mount Washington College, All Baltimore, Newark, Washington, Cincinnati, St. Louis, All St. Louis, Philadelphia, Fall River Rovers, and Brooklyn. The last match takes place at Brooklyn on 15 November next.

The names of the members of the party have already been given in our columns.

They are:—F. H. Milnes, Sheffield captain; C. Coopland, Sheffield; W. Stancer, Sheffield; R. M. Lemoine, Shepherd's Bush; J. J. Bayley, Clapton; H. A. Littlewort, Fulham; A. K. Campbell, Glossop; G. Simon, Notts; E. J. Cotton, Nunhead; T. T. Fitchie, Glossop and Woolwich Arsenal; W. Davidson, Falkirk; G. R. Hoare, Woolwich Arsenal; J. A. Eastwood, Ilford; J. Brown-Sim, Queen's Park; and W. Cleminson, Darlington.

C. COOPLAND.

Inside left forward, who first played for Hillsbro' Board School, and had much to do with that school securing several trophies. Afterwards played for Sheffield Wednesday, Sheffield Club, and Glossop.

F. H. MILNES.

Captain of the side. Can play anywhere. Has assisted many clubs, and is now on the registered playing strength of Glossop. Assisted Sheffield Club when they won the Amateur Cup. Is virtually responsible for the promotion of these American football trips.

W. STANCER.

One of the half backs of the party. Plays for Sheffield Club and Rotherham Town.

The three Sheffield FC players to be selected for the Pilgrims tour. Fred Milnes (centre). C Coopland and W. Stanser.

producing teams which would visit England for international play."

In the *New York Herald*, Milnes added: "Four years ago we came here to this country as missionaries in what we sincerely believe to be a good cause. We have been more than pleased over the satisfactory reports of the steady advance of your players since then. Who knows but we may have something to learn from our transatlantic cousins."

The 1909 touring team played 22 games in just 45 days between October 2 and November 16, winning 16 and losing only twice. They travelled to a number of places including New York, Washington, Boston, Baltimore, Newark, Cincinnati, Chicago, St Louis, Philadelphia and Brooklyn.

St. Louis was a relative hotbed of soccer in the United States and this may explain why the Pilgrims ventured so far west. After easily defeating a select eleven in Philadelphia by 9-0, they were defeated 2-1 in Fall River by a local team by the name of Rovers.

The home side prided themselves on fielding

teams comprised of native born players and adopted an 'American' style, one which we would recognise today as resembling a 'long ball' or 'direct' style of play.

The Pilgrims, who played in white shirts, dark blue shorts and dark blue socks, also beat an All American side 4-0 to win the Cochrane Cup on 30 October 1909 at Sportsman's Park, St Louis. The Cochrane Cup, which possessed a value of $1,500, was seen as the main competition during the US tour.

Interest in soccer was noted when an estimated crowd of 6,000 people turned up to watch the Pilgrims beat an All Chicago side 3-0 in Chicago. Some supporters travelled more than 500 miles just to watch the Pilgrims.

Milnes said at the end of the tour: "I must say that they [the Pilgrims players] devoted the whole of their talents to showing the Americans how the game should be played as a scientific and skilful pastime.

"You can take it from me that the 'soccer' game has come to stay in America."

Back in the United Kingdom, Sheffield FC enjoyed a number of tournaments in a variety of locations. At Easter, 1890, Club travelled to Saltburn-by-the-Sea to play Stockton, Whitby, Darlington, Loftus and Scarborough. Sheffield, captained by William F Beardshaw, won three and drew two of the games.

Club also enjoyed four games in the Portsmouth area in South Hants during April 1908. They followed this trip south with matches in the Channel Islands against Guernsey, Alderney and Jersey teams in April 1909 and again in March 1910.

Waring Stanser was their captain during the Easter visit to the Channel Islands in 1910.

Sheffield FC line up to take on Eindhoven Football Club in Holland in June 1947. Third from left is Frank Pashley, while Bill Mullins is fourth from right. (Pauline Reynolds image).

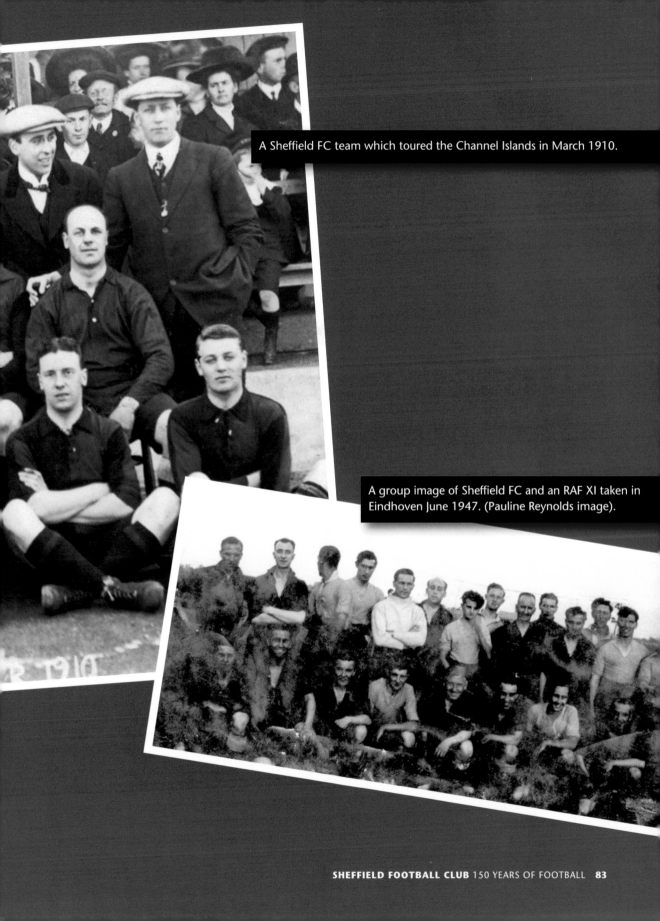

A Sheffield FC team which toured the Channel Islands in March 1910.

A group image of Sheffield FC and an RAF XI taken in Eindhoven June 1947. (Pauline Reynolds image).

Pilgrims' Tour results – 1905

Date	Opponents	Score	Venue	Attendance
09.09.05	Montreal	4-0		
	Hamilton	8-2		
12.09.05	Niagara Falls	5-0	Niagara Falls	
13.09.05	Berlin Rangers	1-2	Berlin	2000
16.09.05	Galt	3-3	Galt	4000
18.09.05	Peninsulars	10-2	Detroit	
	St. Louis	10-0		
	St. Louis	6-0		
	Chicago	4-1		
01.10.05	Chicago	1-2		
	Philadelphia	5-0		
	Philadelphia	4-1		
	Philadelphia	5-0		
	Boston	5-0		
	Fall River	4-3		
	New York	7-1		
24.10.05	Pennsylvania Univ.	10-0	Philadelphia	

Played: 17, Won: 14, Drawn: 1, Lost: 2, For: 92, Against: 17.

Tour results – 1909

Date	Opponents	Score	Venue	Attendance
02.10.09	All New York	4-0	Livingston	1200
05.10.09	Sons of St. George	13-0	Baltimore	400
07.10.09	Mount Washington	14-0	Baltimore	700
09.10.09	Scots-Americans	5-0	Newark	4000
12.10.09	Trenton	2-1	Trenton	500
14.10.09	Cincinnati	9-0	Cincinnati	1000
16.10.09	Blue Bells	5-0	St. Louis	1600
17.10.09	St. Theresa's	10-1	St. Louis	2057
20.10.09	Gillespie Thistle	1-1	Gillespie	500
23.10.09	Hyde Park Blues	8-2	Chicago	700
24.10.09	All Chicago	3-0	Chicago	6000
26.10.09	Coal City Maroons	0-0	Coal City	450
30.10.09	All Westerns	4-0	St. Louis	1200
31.10.09	St. Leo's	13-1	St. Louis	4300
02.11.09	Philadelphia Cricket	3-0	Philadelphia	1500
04.11.09	Hibernians	0-1	Philadelphia	1077
06.11.09	Pennsylvania	9-0	Philadelphia	4586
10.11.09	Fall River Rovers	1-1	Fall River	2821
13.11.09	Fall River Rovers	1-2	Fall River	3965
14.11.09	New York Amateurs	2-2	Brooklyn	1200
16.11.09	Crescent AC	6-1	Brooklyn	450

Played: 22, Won: 16, Drawn: 4, Lost: 2, For: 124, Against: 13.

The following pictures are from FC Eindhoven's visit to Sheffield in August 1946, two months after Sheffield sent a representative team to the Netherlands. (Pictures courtesy of FC Eindhoven)

1e Wedstrijd
Sted. Elftal Sheffield – Sted. Elftal Eindh. 0–2
Aug 1946

Eindhoven—Sheffield
juni 1946

The Road to Wembley

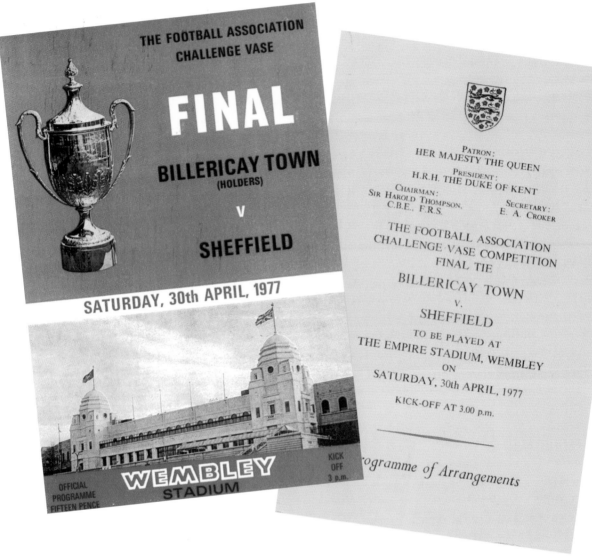

'We're on our way to Wembley!' That was the shout as Sheffield Football Club progressed to the final of the FA Challenge Vase on 30 April 1977 to make their first ever visit to England's most prestigious football stadium.

Cup winners for first time

The Sheffield FC team which reached the final of the FA Vase. Back row (from left to right): Andrew Lodge, Chris Gilbody, Rod Skelton, Steve Hardisty, Mick Wing, John Pugh. Front row (from left to right): Harry Strutt, John Thornhill, Peter Kay, Dave Watts (captain), Howard Haines, Doug Travis.

IT WAS A remarkable achievement by an amateur side to reach the final where they faced the current holders, Billericay Town. The previous year Billericay had become only the second team to win this new piece of silverware, established in the 1974/75 season.

The FA Vase had taken over from the Amateur Cup, which had been scrapped by the FA with many amateur players in the country now receiving payment for playing.

The game was seen as a David versus Goliath final. Sheffield had been playing in the Yorkshire

League since before World War Two, even dropping down to the Third Division at one stage. But they had begun a revival and at the time of the final were challenging for a place in Division One and a County Senior Cup honour.

Billericay were founder-members of the Essex Senior League and in six seasons had won the Championship three times. Progressing to the Athenian League in 1977, Billericay continued their success by winning the League Championship and the League Cup in their first season. They were clear favourites to lift the FA Vase.

Joint managers of the Sheffield FC team at the time were Chris Stanley and Roy Ford. Chris and Roy had both played for the club during the 1950s and had returned to mastermind the recent revival.

Sheffield FC had to battle their way through seven rounds to reach the final and below is a run-down of how they enjoyed the route to Wembley.

Round 1 – Tadcaster Albion, won 4-1 (home)
Round 2 – Clitheroe, won 2-1 (home)
Round 3 – Arnold Kingswell, won 4-2 (home)
Round 4 – Friar Lane O.B, won 2-0 (home)
Round 5 – Anson Villa, won 3-0 (home)
Round 6 – East Ham United, won 4-0 (away)
Semi-final First leg – Barton Rovers, won 2-0 (home)
Second leg – Barton Rovers, drew 1-1 (away). Won 3-1 on aggregate.

The team which took Sheffield FC to the final had an average age of 22 and included men from all walks of life including, a steel worker, an accountant and a builder. Below are the notes on

A Sheffield FC side from 1977, in front of the stand at Abbeydale Park. (left to right) Back row – Roy Ford, Steve Gillam, Steve Hardisty, John Pugh, Malcolm Wheatley (chairman), Mick Wing, Chris Gilbody, John Thornhill, Chris Stanley and Dave Moxon. Seated – Andy Lodge, Lennie Yates, Howard Haines, Rod Skelton, Doug Travis, Harry Strutt and Pete Kay.

the squad from the FA Challenge Vase Wembley match programme.

Mick Wing

Goalkeeper, aged 22. Made one appearance at Wembley before, having once represented Sheffield Youth Clubs at the stadium. Joined Sheffield FC from Oaks Fold Youth Club in 1974. Education Officer.

Chris Gilbody

Defender, aged 23. Began as a midfield player before being converted into a successful full-back. Joined Sheffield after playing in the local works league. Publicity representative.

Andrew Lodge

Defender, aged 19. Promoted to the first team midway through the previous season. A versatile player who likes to attack from defence and is also effective in midfield. Clerk.

Steve Hardisty

Defender, aged 24. A former Rotherham United player, who is now in his third spell with Sheffield, having also played for Boston United. Travels 20 miles to home fixtures. Steelworker.

Dave Watts

Defender, aged 26. Captain and oldest member of the squad. Began at Sheffield United and had spells with Buxton, Worksop and Frickley before taking his experience to Sheffield. Works as a foreman.

Rod Skelton

Midfielder, aged 24. Now in his third season at Sheffield since joining from a local junior side where he scored 60 goals in one season! Accountant.

Peter Kay

Striker, aged 21. Joined Sheffield after standing in to make up a tour party to Ostend last summer. An experienced player despite his young age. Computer programmer.

Sheffield FC's John Pugh challenges for the ball in the FA Vase final at Wembley. Sheffield FC are playing in the long sleeves and Umbro diamond on the top of the socks. (Photo courtesy of Peter Roscoe, Sheffield)

Sheffield FC's Pete Kay is surrounded by Billericay players in the FA Vase final. (Photo courtesy of Peter Roscoe, Sheffield)

Striker John Thornhill with the Sheffield FC supporters in the background at Wembley. (Photo courtesy of Peter Roscoe, Sheffield)

John Thornhill
Striker, aged 24. Top scorer for Sheffield in the competition with seven goals. He netted all three in both legs of the semi-final against Barton. Began his career with Barnsley and had spells with several Northern Premier League sides before joining Sheffield in 1975. Steelworker.

Howard Haines
Striker, aged 25. A former amateur player with Sheffield United, he joined Sheffield FC six years ago. Club jester. He can also play at full-back. Paper merchant's representative.

Harry Strutt
Striker, aged 22. His second appearance at Wembley, having also played there for Sheffield Youth Clubs. Trialist with Sheffield Wednesday, he played for the same youth club as keeper Mick Wing. Lorry driver.

Doug Travis
Striker, aged 23. Currently in his second spell with Club having also played for Winterton. A strong runner, he has had trials for several professional clubs. Builder.

John Pugh
Striker, aged 24. Joined Sheffield in 1975 after assisting several clubs. Scored six goals on the way to Wembley. Polytechnic lecturer.

Len Yates

Striker, aged 18. Youngest member of the squad. He joined Sheffield last summer from Sheffield United where he was a junior. Len broke a leg against Clitheroe in the second round of the FA Vase, but is now back to peak form. Apprentice toolmaker.

It had been a financial struggle to get the team to Wembley, but the club were determined not to miss out on the opportunity. An appeal was run in the *Sheffield Star* newspaper to help generate around £3,500 to help the team travel to London.

The club stayed at the well-known Hendon Hall Hotel and each player was even kitted out in matching blazers provided by a supporter. Sheffield FC were intent on making the most of the occasion – this was after all their Cup final.

More than 12,000 people were at the game with about 3,000 supporters travelling from Sheffield to support Club. A contingent even included Sheffield United fans who had decided to watch Sheffield FC instead of the Blades' league game at Chelsea!

Sheffield FC, who were given the south dressing room, rose to the occasion and matched their more experienced rivals, securing a credible 1-1 draw. It was left to lecturer John Pugh to make history by becoming the first and only player to score at Wembley for Club.

The replay took place at Nottingham Forest's City Ground just four days later, but despite the continued heroics from Sheffield, Billericay won 2-1, with John Thornhill scoring Club's consolation.

All the Sheffield FC players received a gold runners-up medal from the Football Association as a reward for their remarkable achievement.

Looking back at the historic event 30 years later, Chris Stanley who was manager of Sheffield FC at the time of the final, said: "The trip to Wembley was a great day out and a fantastic occasion.

"We had a great team at the time. It was well-balanced with a number of players having the ability to win a game. They all gave 100 per cent every week, even in training. I was proud to be a part of the club and to work with those players."

Sheffield FC recovered from the disappointment by going on to reach Division One in the Yorkshire League with their second successive promotion.

A year later in 1978, Club also clinched the Yorkshire League Cup for the first time in their history with an emphatic 4-1 win against Maltby Miners Welfare at Bramall Lane.

Maltby had taken the lead, but Sheffield FC responded with Steve Hardisty's shot deflecting past keeper Hinchcliffe.

Andrew Lodge then put Club in front with a well-taken header in the 53rd minute, before Keiron Miles and John Pugh each added a goal late on to seal victory.

A newspaper clipping of Sheffield FC's visit to Wembley – dated April 30 1977. (*Sheffield Newspapers Ltd*)

Unique Opponents

It would be a fair assessment to say that Sheffield FC has probably played more games than most teams in the world. And, as a club with a long history, it is no surprise that they have come up against some unique opponents during those 150 years.

In this section, we take a look at the teams Sheffield FC have played both on a friendly and competitive basis.

A team photo of a Sheffield FC side from 1993, which played in a Sheffield City centenary game against Queen's Park.(Picture from match programme).Back row (from left to right): A. Murboosh, M. Casey, J. Flynn, J. Machin, G. Walker, D. Lomas, M. Walshaw, M. Pass, R. Parkes, J. Swann, K. Johnson (Manager) and R. Jackson (Assistant Manager) Front row (from left to right): J. Ransford, D. Kenney, R. Peacock, J. Pearson, N. Brown (captain), G. Barnsley, C. Worsford and G. Mitchell.

Club v Queen's Park

Sheffield FC has enjoyed a long-standing relationship with Queen's Park, the oldest club in Scotland, with a number of games taking place between the two sides. The relationship undoubtedly stems from the fact that both clubs have continued to retain their amateur status.

The contests even became a regular event in the clubs' calendar, with the relationship reaffirmed when Queen's Park agreed to send a team to play in Sheffield FC's centenary celebrations in 1957. More details of this can be found in the centenary chapter.

SHEFFIELD UNITED

Amateur *Match*

SHEFFIELD F.C.
VERSUS
PEGASUS F.C.

BRAMALL LANE GROUND
SATURDAY, 27th DECEMBER, 1952
KICK-OFF 2.15 p.m.

OFFICIAL PROGRAMME - - - - TWO PENCE

A more recent game between Sheffield FC and Queen's Park took place on 27 April 1993, at Sheffield Wednesday's Hillsborough stadium. The match formed part of the City of Sheffield's centenary celebrations.

This was a good time for Sheffield football, with the game taking place in the same month as both Wednesday and United reached the FA Cup semi-final at Wembley.

Current president Alan Methley, chairman of Sheffield FC at that time, said: "When it was suggested that a special football match should be a part of the Sheffield Centenary celebrations, no one looked any further than a resumption of the historic rivalry between the oldest clubs in England and Scotland, ourselves and our great friends from Queen's Park."

At the time Sheffield FC were playing their home matches at Don Valley Stadium, with Kenny 'Jock' Johnson, a former Club player, now the team manager. Jock had experience with Sheffield Wednesday and Newcastle United and in non-league with Matlock Town. He took over in May 1992.

Club v Pegasus

Ahead of Sheffield FC's centenary celebrations, the club played a unique game against Pegasus at Bramall Lane, on 27 December 1952.

The match saw the oldest club take on the youngest senior amateur side of the time.

Pegasus was formed in 1948 and included players drawn from Oxford and Cambridge Universities. They were enjoying a tour of the north during the Christmas and New Year period.

Pegasus were one of the best known amateur clubs, winning the FA Amateur Cup the previous season after beating Bishop Auckland 2-1 at Wembley in front of 100,000 people – a record for an amateur game.

A crowd of 11,168 turned up at Sheffield United's ground to watch Pegasus win 8-1 – the visitors scoring four goals in a frantic six-minute spell. Keith Smith netted Club's only goal just after the hour mark following an Alan Pashley free-kick.

It was the development of teams such as Pegasus and the Corinthian Casuals which helped stimulate interest in amateur football. Even though more people were watching the game than playing it, there still remained an increase in the number of amateur clubs being formed.

Club v Wimbledon

Most teams in non-league football will admit to dreaming of successive promotions and eventually rising to the top division in English football. For many this remains a dream – but not for Wimbledon FC.

The club had spent most of its history outside the Football League, until a rapid rise saw them reach the First Division, now the Premiership, during the 1980s and a famous FA Cup final win over Liverpool at Wembley.

Sheffield FC met the Dons on their successful climb when the clubs crossed paths in a FA Amateur Cup tie at Hillsborough on 28 January 1950.

Wimbledon, who at the time were playing at Plough Lane, competed in the Isthmian League and were quite a successful amateur club. They had won the Isthmian League and the Surrey Senior Cup four times and the London Senior Cup twice.

In the programme notes before the game, Sheffield FC wrote: "Since 1904, when we won the FA Amateur Cup, we have been privileged to partake in matches of this calibre.

"Here in South Yorkshire we are firmly convinced there is a necessary talent from which we can build such a team and we have a go-ahead policy to that end.

"Our lads, some of who you know quite well, have been looking forward to the game ever since the draw and, though this is a great occasion for most of them, they are confident of making a determined effort to take the game. They are capable of some very good football and have trained hard from the start."

Club put up a good fight, but were beaten 3-2 in an exciting game.

Club v World Club Champions

Sheffield FC have played against some illustrious teams during their 150-year history, including the first ever 'World Cup' Champions. Who is this you might ask, Juventus, Real Madrid or even Manchester United? All wrong, the answer is West Auckland Town in Durham.

Club played West Auckland Town in the FA Cup, losing 4-0 on 31 August 2002.

West Auckland represented Great Britain in the inaugural 'World Cup' during the Easter of 1910 in Turin, Italy. The competition was sponsored by millionaire Sir Thomas Lipton after he was made Knight of the Grand Order of Italy.

His name was put forward for the silverware and the Sir Thomas Lipton trophy was the first unofficial World Club Cup.

Various stories abound of how West Auckland were chosen to represent the United Kingdom. One

A match programme from Sheffield FC's game with Wimbledon.

LUCKY PRIZE DRAW NO: / 001489

·CITY OF SHEFFIELD· CENTENARY·

Sheffield Football Club

V

Queens Park

HILLSBOROUGH, SHEFFIELD

Tuesday 27th April 1993 7.50 kick off

MATCH SPONSOR

Sondico

Souvenir Program £1

A match programme from Sheffield FC's game with Queen's Park during Sheffield's 100 years celebrations.

tells of how the Football Association had declined to nominate a team but Sir Thomas insisted a side from this own country needed to take part. One of his employees was a referee in the Northern League and was instrumental in helping to choose West Auckland.

Others include how Juventus, who also played a role in developing the event, believed the initials WAFC stood for Woolwich Arsenal Football Club!

The West Auckland side was made up mainly of coal miners who struggled to raise the money to make the trip to Italy. Some even pawned possessions to do so. Amazingly, the team of unknown

amateurs went on to beat FC Stuttgart 2-0 and then FC Winterthur of Switzerland 2-0 in the final at the Turin Stadium on 12 April 1910.

To show the triumph was no fluke, West Auckland retained the trophy the following season, beating Juventus 6-1 in Italy on 17 April 1911. A Channel Four film, 'A Captain's Tale,' starring Dennis Waterman, re-told the story.

In January 1994, the 3ft silver Sir Thomas Lipton trophy was stolen. A replica was made by a Sheffield silversmith named Jack Spencer who produced a £20,000 trophy working from photos and videos.

Annual Dinners

It has been a tradition of Sheffield Football Club to mark the anniversary of its formation with an annual dinner every October.

This has taken place each year, with the most notable being the centenary celebrations in 1957 at the Cutlers' Hall in Sheffield, attended by the Duke of Edinburgh. More details can be found in a separate chapter of this book.

Cllr Peter Price, deputy leader of Sheffield City Council, Derek Dooley, Ron Scaife, ex-club president, Emlyn Hughes, Nobby Stiles and Keith Healey, president of the club, at the Sheffield FC annual dinner, October 1989. (*Sheffield Newspapers*)

THE CLUB'S jubilee dinner was also a prestigious event 50 years earlier, with several key figures from the club's history speaking, including the co-founder Col. Nathaniel Creswick.

Held at the Victoria Hotel, Sheffield on Monday 4 November 1907, more than 110 guests were present and Creswick told several stories linked to the club, most of which were anecdotal.

The *Sheffield Telegraph* on 5 November 1907 reported him as saying that:

'William Prest and himself, when it was decided to form the club, went for a walk into the country to decide what rules of football they should use. They wrote to the leading public schools, Eton, Harrow, Winchester, Westminster, Rugby, and some others, and obtained a lot of different rules. (Laughter).

'One rule he remembered, he believed it came form Winchester, was that you should not hold and hack [kick indiscriminately] a man at the same time (Loud laughter).

'The number of players and the hours of play in those days were unlimited, they played generally until it was dark. One match he remembered was against Norton, when they played four against six for four hours. He was one of the four and he remembered that he became very personal. (Laughter).

'There was another match played at Sheffield Barracks; it was originally agreed to play twenty-a-side, but after they had been playing some time he thought there were a few too many on the opposite side, so he asked the captain of the soldiers' team to parade his men and count them. He did so and it was found there were thirty-eight of them. (Laughter). The first time they went to play Nottingham it was a twelve-a-side match and he was pleased to say seven of the Sheffield twelve were still alive. (Applause).'

Another landmark year was the 125th anniversary in 1982, with the annual dinner attended by Football Association chairman Sir Bert Millichip at the club's Abbeydale Park ground.

Sheffield FC also organised an exhibition game against Manchester United at Bramall Lane to mark the occasion. Ron Atkinson was the manager at Manchester United, who had finished third in Division One, now the Premiership, the previous season. Lou Macari was the only senior player in the team, which also featured a young and then unknown Mark Hughes.

Former Sheffield United player Paddy Buckley was Club's manager and at the time of the game, Sheffield FC occupied second place in the First Division of the Northern Counties East League.

In his programme notes for the game, Paddy said: "Tonight the young players of Sheffield Club will be pitting their skills against the giants of the game. For them, this is the Big One and I know they'll be giving me 100 per cent effort as they have done all season.

"Their record this year deserves a mention. At the present time we are unbeaten in our last seven league games and have amassed a tally of 19 goals for and 11 against."

The Sheffield FC side also included four guest players, Emlyn Hughes then manager of Rotherham United, Tony Currie from QPR, Terry Curran who at the time was playing for Sheffield United and Blades manager Ian Porterfield.

Over the years, the annual dinners became an important event for Sheffield FC, allowing the club to raise money through ticket sales and a football auction on the night.

A host of well-known names from the game have given their support by attending the events, helping to ensure a high attendance and valuable publicity for the club in the local media.

At the 128th annual dinner on October 24th 1985, former Juventus and Wales international John Charles was the chief guest, along with former England keeper, Gordon Banks and ex-Leeds United star Peter Lorimer.

World Cup winner Banks must have enjoyed his

A match programme from Sheffield FC's 125th anniversary game against Manchester United in 1982.

A Sheffield FC first team from 1982 when the club marked its 125th anniversary with a game against Manchester United.

evening as he returned the following year. This time he was joined by guests from Sheffield United, including chairman Reg Brearley, managing director Derek Dooley and team manager Billy McEwan.

Sheffield-born FA Cup final referee Keith Hackett was also there, as were representatives from Queen's Park FC.

Sheffield FC secured a major coup for their 130th annual dinner in October 1987 at the Baldwins Omega when the top guest was Bobby Robson, then England manager.

Robson had been involved in Sheffield FC's centenary celebrations 30 years earlier when he played and scored for the England B side at Hillsborough as part of the anniversary events.

More recently, Robson continued his support for the club by agreeing to become a Sheffield FC member. Another World Cup winner Nobby Stiles, and ex-England and Liverpool captain Emlyn

Hughes were the chief guests at the 132nd annual dinner event.

On that occasion, former Sheffield FC president Ron Scaife was presented with a plaque from the Football Association in recognition of his 50 years service which stretched back to when he was a player with the club before the Second World War.

A year later, another member of the 1966 England World Cup team was in attendance, the late Alan Ball, who died in April 2007

One of the most prestigious chief guests to attend a Sheffield FC annual dinner was Sir Stanley Matthews in 1991.

On occasions some of the guests were invited to give a speech to the audience. During one Club dinner the guest speaker was former England, Everton, Arsenal and Sheffield United Joe Mercer, who finished his toast to the club by saying: "Don't forget, the game is all about the players."

Tough Times for Club

As football entered the mid-1980s, the advent of television rights and multi-million pound transfer deals were set to be unleashed in a new phase for the game.

THE COUNTRY'S leading clubs and players were about to enjoy one of the most prosperous and lucrative times ever in football – a situation which continues today.

It was, however, a very different story at the other end of the football scale, particularly for those clubs outside the Football League. Finances were tight and, if decisions to invest went wrong, the future of the whole club would be hanging in the balance.

The best way to stay in the black was for the team to be successful. In the 1985/86 season both Sheffield FC's senior teams were performing well, with the reserve side promoted to the Premier Division of the Whitbread County Senior League.

Meanwhile, the first team finished second in the First Division of the Northern Counties East League but were denied promotion because their home ground at Abbeydale Park did not meet the required standard for that level of football.

This was not to be the last time the club would find itself in this predicament and the disappointment was followed with the departure of manager Bud Evans to Denaby United.

The achievements on the field were a boost to the club, but Sheffield FC were being hit off it by the realities of running a football club in the Northern Counties East League.

In a report to the club's annual general meeting on 25 May 1989, Alan Methley, who at the time was responsible for promotions and publicity, wrote: "The club simply does not have enough 'bodies' in all departments of its activities to move it into the next decade. I have to say that if this problem is not solved the Club will eventually fold."

As with any organised outfit, there were costs involved in running the club. Cash had to be found each season for ground rent and maintenance, travel expenses, kit expenses, coach hire, medical fees, and match-day refreshments. Even corner flags were an expense as pitch costs increased.

In the 1996/97 season the club's expenses had reached approximately £30,000 for the year and with income around the same figure, it was often a difficult balancing act to limit any financial losses.

To make ends meet, Sheffield FC had to rely on money coming in from gate receipts, matchday raffles, programme sales, sponsorship, merchandise, the annual dinner and donations.

A story in a Sheffield newspaper in January 1992 highlighted the concern over the club's future after the reporter had interviewed Sheffield FC's commercial manager Kevin Smith:

'Kevin appealed for individuals and businesses to come forward with match ball sponsorship and programme advertising.

He said: "We will do everything to keep the club going, but unless we get this support there is a fear it could close. We are the oldest club in the world and it would be very sad if it had to close.

"The problem is we are not getting the support of the people of Sheffield. You can ask people where Sheffield FC play and they just don't know.'"

Sheffield Wednesday and Sheffield United often played their part by donating memorabilia for auctions and staging bucket collections at games, but these were not long-term options.

Attendance at Sheffield FC's home games had dwindled, even though the team was still relatively successful on the field. The attraction of watching Premiership football at both Wednesday and United was proving difficult to compete with.

An anonymous letter to the Sheffield *Green'Un* newspaper in February 1994 summed up the state of affairs. It read: "One of the most disquieting aspects of the local soccer scene is the apparent apathy shown by the Sheffield public towards our oldest football team Sheffield FC.

"Cash strapped, the club's Don Valley stadium future uncertain, shunted around over the last ten years or so from previous home bases at Abbeydale Park and Hillsborough Park, they are now having their best season for years with an excellent chance of winning the North East Counties Premier League title and a Sheffield Senior Cup.

"Crowds at the Don Valley Stadium however are derisory, the away support

Oldest football club set to shut

THE world's oldest football club, Sheffield FC, may face the final whistle after nearly 125 years because of a cash crisis.

The club, which was formed back in October 1857 and is a founder member of the FA, has enough money to scrape through this season.

But staff at the cash-strapped side, which has been attracting only 50 people to recent home matches, fear it may close next season.

Commercial manager, Kevin Smith estimates about £8,000 will have to be raised to meet running costs such as ground rent and new its.

By Malcolm Jones

there is the fear it could close,' he said.

"We are 100 per cent convinced this is the oldest club in the world and it would be very sad if it had to close.

"The problem is we are not getting the support the people of Sheffield. You can ask people who Sheffield FC play and they just don't know.'

The club plays home games in the North Counties East League Premier Division at the Don Valley Stadium, but next season moves to nearby Woodburn Road.

Problem

He appealed for individuals and businesses to come forward with match ball sponsorship and programme advertising.

"We will do everything to keep the club going, but unless we get this support

Anyone who can help with support for Sheffield FC should contact Mr Smith on Sheffield 853364.

Mr Smith is now organising a raffle — and appealing for ticket outlets.

His daughters Michelle, aged 14, and Lynette, four, will be doing a sponsored swim next month.

● Wham and blast: P10:11

nearly always embarrassingly outnumbering the few Club supporters who turn up on a regular basis.

"Maybe the explanation is this transient characteristic which contrasts starkly with its long standing rival Hallam FC whose support has remained loyal and reasonably large, consistent perhaps with the team's regular home base at Sandygate."

When Alan Methley was elected President of Sheffield FC in October 1995, the club had debts in the region of £17,000. The situation sparked a reorganisation of the club with a new company established to run the finances and underwrite the debt.

Peter Beeby, who also took over as chairman, told the *Sheffield Star* at the time, that despite balancing its books the previous year the club's debts were causing real problems. He said: "Major changes were necessary. The investment in the club was essential but we believe we have an under-marketed potential."

Officials at the club began to push for new streams of income, with the top priority being to secure a stabilised home ground. This would help create further sponsorship opportunities and a long-term base to build support on the terraces.

Before long, Sheffield FC made the move to its current ground in Dronfield and began to further utilise its unique position as the oldest club in the world. Alan Methley's earlier suggestion of more bodies was acted upon with a number of volunteers in place to help with the running of the club on all levels, both during the week and on match-days.

Dark clouds hung over the club during those tough days, but now a new era was dawning for Sheffield FC and they were able to look forward to the 21st century with a certain amount of optimism.

FIFA Order of Merit

Sheffield Football Club's fortunes both on and off the field began to change once the club had established a base on Sheffield Road, Dronfield, next to the Coach and Horses pub.

The move, in April 2001, allowed the club to lay the foundations for a more certain future and bring to an end the stadium troubles which had plagued them since leaving Abbeydale more than 15 years earlier.

Sheffield FC chairman Richard Tims received a personal invitation from Barcelona president Joan Laporte to the Nou Camp.

CLUB'S SWITCH to the new ground coincided with the team winning the Northern Counties East League Cup for the first time, beating First Division Gedling Town. Despite the atrocious conditions, Sheffield FC ran out 2-1 winners, with goals from Jon Pickess and Mickey Stewart.

Another key development in that year was the appointment of Richard Tims as chairman. He had previously been a Director at the club and took over the top job from Peter Beeby.

Richard quickly developed a number of sponsorship schemes for businesses to get involved and help make Sheffield FC more self-sufficient. The cost of running a football club continued to be high and with the move to a new ground now complete, new expenditures were created making finances tighter than ever.

Sheffield FC chairman Richard Tims was Invited by the Catalan Football Federation to attend an awards ceremony recognising the Club's unique achievement.

The club could no longer just rely on gate receipts as a way to generate income and Richard had to create new revenue streams in order for Sheffield FC to survive.

In an effort to promote the club and boost sponsorship support from businesses, Richard requested the Football Association officially recognise Sheffield FC as the world's first football club in writing. The FA duly responded and with backing from the country's governing body now behind them, Sheffield FC were able to take a massive step forwards.

As this book was written, Sheffield FC has the support of 54 sponsors, the highest ever amount in the club's history and likely to be on par with many Football League clubs.

The list includes a host of companies, both small and large, local to international brands, but all providing much needed funding for the club. Their backing enables Sheffield FC to reach its 150th season and celebrate this special anniversary.

Following the announcement from the English FA in 2003, Sheffield FC received an invitation from the Catalan Football Federation to attend an event celebrating the history of football.

More than 2,000 dignitaries from more than 400 clubs were at the prestigious ceremony, including Chairman Richard, who was presented with an accolade in recognition of Sheffield FC's unique position as the world's first football club.

The award had put Sheffield FC into the international spotlight and Richard was asked by Barcelona president Joan Laporte to visit the Nou Camp, where he was given a personal tour of the world-renowned venue from the club's chief.

Richard said: "It was quite a surreal trip, Laporte was fascinated about Sheffield FC and he wanted to know everything about our history. To have one of the most well-known and successful figures from the world of football take such a huge interest in our small non-league club was just amazing.

A German film crew from Spiegel TV filmed a documentary on the world's oldest football club.

The Order of Merit medal presented to Sheffield FC by FIFA in 2004.

"It inspired me to take the club forward locally, nationally and internationally. What we had was very special and we needed to start telling the world about our unique football club to help create additional financial support."

The trip to Spain was to be the first of many excursions onto the continent for the club, but the biggest of them all arrived in 2004 when Sheffield FC were invited to the centennial celebrations of the Fédération Internationale de Football Association in Paris.

FIFA, the football world's governing body, was formed in 1904 – the same year Sheffield FC clinched the FA Amateur Cup – and to mark its 100 years a unique awards ceremony was staged. The world's greatest living players, clubs and officials attended, along with Richard.

Sheffield FC and Spanish giants Real Madrid CF were presented with a FIFA Centennial Order of Merit, the only two clubs ever to receive this award from FIFA.

Richard recalls: "I remember sitting down at the awards hall on the front row alongside people like Bobby Charlton, Franz Beckenbauer, Pele and Alfredo Di Stefano. It was just surreal that a lad from Sheffield would be here amongst all these greats.

"Sepp Blatter was presenting the awards and he told everyone how FIFA had a special award for two unique clubs. Before I knew it I was on stage with Blatter and Real Madrid´s Emilio Butragueño."

Following on from the order of merit, Sheffield FC's union with

Sheffield FC chairman Richard Tims is presented with the Order of Merit by FIFA President Sepp Blatter.

Real Madrid started to blossom and Richard and club director Simon Webster met with Real Madrid´s vice-president Emilio Butragueño, who showed them around the magnificent Santiago Bernabéu stadium.

The reason for the visit was to create a partnership between the world's first club and the world's greatest and most successful club.

During his trip to Madrid, Richard commented:

"I would say that there's nothing in the UK that can compare with this stadium. Manchester United´s ground is fantastic, we're rebuilding Wembley at the moment, which is going to be magnificent, and there's the new Arsenal stadium. But there's a certain atmosphere about this stadium that takes your breath away. Does anyone have a ball nearby?

"We really appreciate that Real Madrid have taken the time to form a partnership with the world's oldest club because we feel it's important for the future of the game.

"Sheffield FC don't play professional football, we play for the love of the game. And in this age this is an achievement. We would like to build partnerships with every football club in the world.

"There are around 305,000 official football clubs and all of them originated from Sheffield FC. I think that every club should have a relationship with the fathers of football."

Meanwhile, Sheffield FC's senior side were enjoying great success completing a cup double by winning both the League Cup and the Sheffield & Hallamshire FA Senior Cup in the 2004/5 season.

It was the second time in four years they had

Sheffield FC chairman Richard Tims and director Simon Webster at Real Madrid's Bernabeu Stadium.

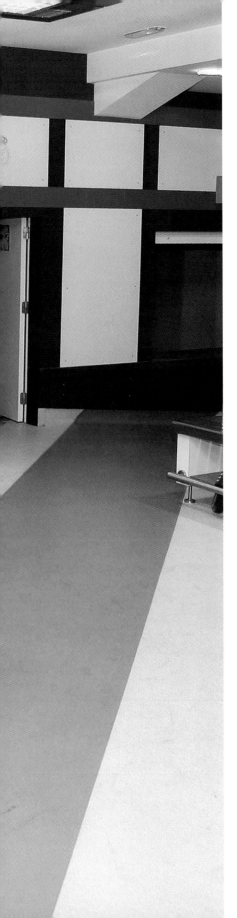

lifted The Northern Counties East League Cup, beating Harrogate Railway 2-1. Two goals in a six-minute spell were enough to hand Club the win.

Ben Cressey's 26th minute free-kick put the defence under pressure and with Harrogate failing to clear effectively, Rob Ward toe-poked the ball into the path of Tom Jones who thundered it into the net.

Sheffield FC extended their lead before the break when Craig Marsh burst through from midfield only to be fouled by Harrogate's Chris Howarth. Marsh took the free-kick quickly before the Harrogate defence could regroup, feeding Chris White who made no mistake.

The teams that day were – Sheffield FC: Bonnington, Hilton, Kontou, Jones, Cressey, Anson, O'Carroll, Marsh, Ward, Cheetham (Holmes), White (Carrington). Sub Not Used: Tevendale.

Harrogate Railway Athletic: Ashforth, Holmes, Haigh, Henderson, Bairstow, Gray, Howarth, L.Ryan, Featherstone (Warburton), Hillier (Day), S.Ryan. Sub Not Used: Stevenson.

A week later, Sheffield FC followed this success by clinching the Sheffield & Hallamshire FA Senior Cup with a victory over Nationwide Conference North Premier Division side Worksop Town at Hillsborough.

It was the first time Sheffield FC had won the trophy for more than a decade and the achievement was a repeat of that 1994 final against Worksop, which Club had won 6-5 on penalties.

The vital goal came in the 89th minute from Ben Cressey. Chris White and substitute Darren Holmes broke down the left, cutting the ball across goal. The Worksop defence failed to clear their lines properly with the ball breaking to Cressey, who fired a half-volley from the edge of the area into the net via the underside of the bar.

Sheffield FC, two divisions lower than Worksop, were the clear underdogs, but they played with the air of a team with nothing to lose and were the better side on the day.

Manager Dave McCarthy said after the game: "I was delighted with the attitude of the boys. They really stuck to the game plan. The result was never in doubt. I was expecting a tough match and I think the best team won on the day."

The sides were – Sheffield FC: Bonnington, Kontou, Cressey, Jones, Marsh, Anson, O'Carroll, Carrington, Ward, Cheetham (Holmes), White. Subs Not Used: Tevendale, Ingall.

Worksop Town: Bowling, Hanson, Davies, O'Callaghan, Jackson, Dudgeon, Wilson, Cleary (Townsend), Bambrook (Payne), Cropper, Norton. Sub Not Used: Nicholson.

Bright Future for Club

Sheffield FC in the new millennium is a club embodying everything good about grassroots football and the positive role it can play in the local area.

Along with increasing sponsorship, Chairman Richard Tims was keen to raise the profile of the world's first football club, particularly in the community.

A ladies team was established for the first time in the club's history after joining forces with Norton Ladies FC and the side started life in 2003 in the Yorkshire and Humberside Premier Division.

Richard said at the time: "We recognise the increasing popularity of women's football in this country and if Sheffield FC can help such a growth and encourage more players to get involved that can only be good for the sport and the local community."

IN THE 2006/07 season the ladies side finished second in the now North East Regional Division One and even caused a cup upset by beating Huddersfield Town, 2-1. Lisa Bailey hit a brace, grabbing the winner four minutes into extra-time. It was arguably the ladies' best ever win as the West Yorkshire side were top of the league above them, the Premier Division.

With the club now enjoying a regular base at Dronfield, a move which later saw Sheffield FC buy their first ever stadium, more teams were allowed to be developed.

A link with AFC Dronfield was created to form a number of junior clubs for many young people of all ages. At the time of writing, Sheffield FC currently has 13 junior teams.

Opportunities to play for the world's first football club continued to be developed and September 2006 saw the creation of an under14s and an under16s girls teams, following the growth of interest in female football.

Both teams play their home games in the Sheffield and Hallamshire Girls County League at Cowley Lane, Holmsfield, close to the first-team's Bright Finance Stadium.

The development of the girls' sides followed the announcement that Sheffield FC'S Under 19s Academy squad was being run in conjunction with Hillsborough College.

Students at the college are given an opportunity to play for the club in the newly formed North Midlands Under-19 Football League against sides

Former England internationals Tony Adams and Paul Bracewell help launch Boots for Africa with chairman Richard Tims.

including Alfreton Town, Dunkirk and Eastwood Town.

Sheffield FC's community development team of Eddie Edwards, Dave McCarthy and Lee Walshaw are also working tirelessly to create a range of programmes raising awareness of sport for all.

This includes coaching for pupils with special needs and learning difficulties at 11 Sheffield schools and centres. They offer football and fitness sessions to youngsters excluded from school or with behavioural problems.

In the summer of 2006, Sheffield FC staged a successful World Cup Day for special needs youngsters from primary and secondary schools and also a friendly game against the Great Britain deaf squad in March 2007 at their Bright Finance Stadium.

The club has established a Football Development Centre and provides coaching as part of the Football Association's Three Lions scheme, as well as coaching camps during the schools holidays.

An affiliation with the Sheffield Association for People with Cerebral Palsy has been developed through Eddie Edwards and together both groups offer a number of activities including football, cricket and boccia at the disability sports and social club on Bawtry Road, Sheffield.

CP Sheffield FC became the first football team to join the boccia national league and club member Jennifer Newby became Senior Boccia National Champion for 2007.

Each week, football coaching is provided through Sheffield FC's two successful disability teams developed from a squad of more than 30 players – with members travelling from Birmingham, Manchester and Leeds to be involved.

Former Sports Minister Richard Caborn has supported the launch of a number of Sheffield FC community activities.

Richard Caborn and Football legend Derek Dooley at the announcement of B Braun Medical becoming a club sponsor.

The two disability teams, one created solely for people with cerebral palsy, have enjoyed great success on the field, beating teams such as Chelsea and Sheffield Wednesday. A number of players were also selected for international honours, including Steve McDonald who represented England against Argentina.

Disability coach Eddie Edwards said:

"It is our intention to get members integrated into the community, helping them to lead a normal life. By bringing people together through sport, we aim to help people understand the disabilities and the difficulties our members have to go through each day.

"We looked at coming under an umbrella with an official football club. All the teams we played against were from professional clubs, such as Liverpool, Everton and Manchester City. We were just known as Eddie's team!

"We had little financial support compared to the others and when our shirts clashed with the opposition we had to turn them inside out as we didn't have any other. The shirts were pink on the inside and nobody wanted to wear it then!

"We looked at joining together with Sheffield Wednesday or Sheffield United, but felt it would end up dividing the support of members.

"We then discovered Sheffield FC and it was a perfect match. Chairman Richard sold me the dream and outlined how we could take the project forward. The club is very much a community club, it is probably one of the busiest in the region for its work with local people. I thought the idea of our disability team being part of the oldest football club in the world was fantastic.

"When we give training sessions, it can be an interesting experience. But it's truly great to see a deaf person, someone with cerebral palsy and another with learning difficulties all playing football together in one team, on one field.

"This is a team of people. We are not here to create elite athletes, but to give our members the confidence they can use in every day life."

All the activities are run through Sheffield FC's Inclusion and Diversity Scheme, which was launched in April 2006 by then Sports Minister Richard Caborn and Natascha Engel MP. The scheme, which will run for at least five years, has been part-funded through a grant from the Football Foundation.

At the launch Mr Caborn said:

"I am delighted to help Sheffield FC launch their Inclusion and Diversity Scheme. Football began here and it is great to see the club continue to develop its community and grassroots work. There should be no barriers to access sport for anyone and schemes like this should be praised.

"The Sheffield FC scheme will help re-emphasise the importance of promoting equal opportunities and diversity in and through football and highlight the positive aspects of sports participation."

Sheffield FC's commitment to community work was recognised when the club was honoured with the Contribution from Industry accolade at the Npower Federation of Disability Sports Awards in Leeds. Club were nominated by healthcare company, B Braun Medical, sponsors of Sheffield FC's disability squad.

One of the biggest campaigns the club has ever been involved in started in May 2006 after chairman Richard returned from a trip to South Africa. Seeing the children play football in their bare feet on rubble-strewn pavements left Richard asking what can be done to build on this love of the game to better the lives of those living in the third world.

It was this moment which sparked Sheffield FC's 'Boots for Africa' campaign to help provide better equipment and facilities for South African children.

Former England and Arsenal defender Tony Adams and BBC Radio Sheffield's Toby Foster helped launched the campaign at the Bright

Finance stadium and to date more than 4,000 pairs of cleaned-up football boots have been supplied to the townships, helping to create the next generation of footballers.

More than 27 schools and colleges, eight local sporting organisations and 28 businesses from across Yorkshire have given their support by having black bin collection points and donating sacks filled with boots.

Almost 12 months to the day since Adams launched the campaign from the Bright Finance

More than 120 local school children attend SoccerJam at the Bright Finance Stadium to raise more than £2,500 for the NSPCC

stadium in Dronfield, the club delivered the first batch of more than 2,500 pairs of boots to youngsters in South Africa.

Richard and officials from South African Sports Trust, the South African High Commission and the South African government attended a special ceremony at the Johannesburg Stadium, where the boots were presented to 17 clubs from townships in South Africa.

The world's first football club then travelled to the township of Soshanguve, situated 45km north of Pretoria, where they were greeted by hundreds of people. To their delight Sheffield FC assistant manager Lee Walshaw held a training session with a group of players before refereeing an 11-a-side game.

Richard said: "The trip was fantastic and enabled the club to achieve what we had set out to do – to provide football boots to youngsters in Africa. It was a very humbling experience and terrific to see football being played everywhere we went and with so much passion.

"To see the boots we collected being distributed to the disadvantaged townships of Africa and seeing the kids' smiling faces was something we will all never forget. This is why we will be extending the campaign until the South African World Cup in 2010 and we will be returning in June with another large collection of boots. The club wants to continue the work we have started here for thousands of young people."

The campaign has again helped put the club on a world-wide scale, reaching out to thousands of people who all share a passion for football.

Another initiative that has enjoyed similar global recognition is the creation of Sheffield FC's membership scheme, which is open to football fans from around the world. Anyone can sign up their support by becoming a member and pay homage to the oldest club.

Members receive tickets to games, regular newsletters, a plaque with their name on at the Bright Finance Stadium, an enamel badge, a certificate and priorities to club events. Around 1,000 people are currently members of Sheffield FC with a number coming from countries outside of the United Kingdom including Spain, Italy, Denmark, Germany, USA, Mauritius and Nigeria.

We have already mentioned in this book some of the illustrious names from the world of football who have become members of the club, from FIFA President Sepp Blatter to rock legends Def Leppard. However Sheffield FC hope every fan of the beautiful game will join the scheme and make them their second favourite club.

Returning to matters on the field, Sheffield FC enjoyed a bit of déjà vu when they scored a dramatic last minute winner to retain the Sheffield and Hallamshire County Senior Cup in May 2006 at Hillsborough. Substitute Rob Ward came off the bench to score and hand Club a 2-1 win over underdogs Parkgate.

Rotherham-based Parkgate had taken an

eight-minute lead when Ryan Johnson poked the ball into the net. However, Sheffield FC levelled the scores on the half hour mark when James Tevendale lobbed advancing Parkgate keeper Lee Manderson following Ryan O'Carroll's free-kick.

In the dying stages of the game, Ward was introduced and in the third minute of injury time, the striker latched on to a Jon Boulter corner to head powerfully past keeper Manderson.

Sheffield FC manager Dave McCarthy said:

"This is a fantastic achievement by the players. They worked hard all night and

got what they deserved in the end. To clinch the trophy for the second year running with a goal in the final minutes is just remarkable. We were pushed all the way by Parkgate who can be proud of the way they played. They were a credit to their management."

The cup final sides were Sheffield FC: Broster, G. Smith, Boulter, Jones, Marsh, Holmes, O'Carroll, Roney (Carrington), P. Smith (Ward), Tevendale, White. Sub Not Used: Hilton.

Parkgate FC: Manderson, Cooper, Lynan (Plant), Colley, Moorwood, Haigh, Outram, Patterson, Cusworth, Gould, Johnson (Turner). Sub Not Used: Dawson.

Sheffield FC turned their attentions to the League Cup Final, but were denied a second double in as many years when they were beaten by Liversedge over the two legs.

In preparation for the 2006/07 season, the oldest football club in the world arranged a pre-season friendly against one of the newest FC United, the Manchester United breakaway team, at Don Valley Stadium on July 29. Club won 1-0.

Team manager Dave McCarthy added Gary Townsend, Chris Dolby, James Holmshaw and

Miles Thorpe to his squad ahead of the new campaign, with the club determined that this would be the year they would win promotion to the Unibond League.

Chris Dolby, a talented midfielder, arrived from Unibond First Division side Belper Town, James Holmshaw, a goalkeeper came from Conference North team Gainsborough Trinity and experienced midfielder Miles Thorpe, was from Conference North side Worksop Town.

McCarthy also added former Sheffield Wednesday striker Vill Powell from Retford United in September and forward David Wilkins joined Club from Arnold Town three months later.

Both made instant impacts with each scoring hat-tricks on their debuts for the club, Powell's in the 5-1 win over Arnold Town and Wilkins' in the 5-0 thumping of Brodsworth MW at the Bright Finance stadium.

Sheffield FC's win against Arnold Town coincided with the start of a terrific run by McCarthy's side who moved clear at the top of the Northern Counties Eastern League Premier Division with a run of 16 wins in 19 league games.

The run had made Sheffield FC favourites to win the title, but one win in the last six games saw them concede top spot to Retford United who had beaten Club twice during those final few games.

Nevertheless, the club's top priority at the start of the campaign had been to win promotion and this was achieved with games to spare – a great achievement in what was a very successful season.

Fittingly, promotion also guaranteed that, in what will be their 150th season, Sheffield FC will compete at their highest ever level. You couldn't have written the script!

Sheffield FC assistant manager Lee Walshaw in South Africa where the club donated more than 2,500 pair of football boots for youngsters.

Football Reaches 150-year Milestone

Football reaches a unique milestone on October 24, 2007 when Sheffield Football Club celebrates its anniversary – 150 years to the day since its formation.

However, celebrations to mark the occasion started at the beginning of the year with the club using the unique event to help promote itself and the work it does locally, nationally and internationally.

SHEFFIELD FC joined forces with the Sheffield Chamber of Commerce, who are also 150 years old, in 2007 so that both organisations could develop a series of events in the city to celebrate the double birthday.

With so much happening in Sheffield during 2007, a new website **www.our150th.co.uk** became operational to keep people up-to-date with events in the year, the major theme focusing on the heritage and innovation of Sheffield.

Sheffield FC began its celebrations by looking back, with eight members of the club's 1957 centenary side invited to watch a league game against Pickering Town at the Bright Finance Stadium.

Norman Cann, who captained the team during the centenary year, was joined by his brother and wing-half Derek, goalkeeper Barry Palfreyman, centre-half Roy Bagworth, winger Pete Copley, inside-right Jack Wasden and inside-forwards Vic Wragg and Pete Havenhand.

Keith Hardie, son of Jim Hardie, who was Sheffield FC secretary when the club marked its 100th anniversary in 1957, also attended the reunion.

On May 2, the day the Chamber marked its birthday, six members of the Chamber's current executive team staged a brief extraordinary meeting in the Lord Mayor's parlour at Sheffield Town Hall, dressed as 1857 business leaders.

It was a faithful re-enactment of the first ever meeting of the Chamber at the same venue 150 years ago. Chairman Richard Tims and manager Dave McCarthy also joined the event and attended dressed as Sheffield FC players from the late 19th Century.

The highlight of the our150th campaign was the joint dinner at Ponds Forge International Sports Centre where stars of showbiz and sport joined top figures from business and politics to write another big headline on the pages of Sheffield's proud history.

In the biggest birthday bash Sheffield had seen for many years, Paul Carrack – ex Squeeze and

Sheffield FC chairman Richard Tims with Roy Bagworth, Keith Hardie son of Jim Hardie, Barry Palfreyman, Norman Cann, Pete Copley, Vic Wragg, Derek Cann, Pete Havenhand and Jack Wasden.

Mike and the Mechanics – performed live and was even joined by Tony Christie for a unique rendition of 'Is This The Way To Amarillo?'

England World Cup winner Sir Bobby Charlton, former Deputy Prime Minister Lord Roy Hattersley and then Sports Minister Richard Caborn were the guest speakers.

In his speech to the 800 strong audience, Sir Bobby said: "I never imagined I would be here speaking at a joint dinner to celebrate 150 years of the oldest football club. It is a great honour to be asked to attend. Sheffield is a proud football city and it's amazing to think such a small club has played such a big influence on the world.

"I have always been fond of Sheffield and played a number of interesting games in the city. I believe that without question Wednesday and United will be back in the Premiership before long.

"Both are traditional football clubs which are run properly, have a great spirit and come from a city with a big heart and a huge fan base – these are the fundamentals any club requires to play in the top flight."

Lord Hattersley, a well-known Sheffield Wednesday supporter, added: "Not many people may believe me when I say that there was a tinge of regret when Sheffield United were relegated from the Premiership.

"Hopefully, next year we will see both teams crossing the finishing line together, hand-in-hand to promotion. Sheffield's two great teams both deserve their place in the Premiership."

Sheffield MPs David Blunkett, Clive Betts, Angela Smith and Nick Clegg were also at the dinner, along with the Lord Lieutenant of South Yorkshire, the Assay Master and the Master Cutler.

Others joining the celebrations included singer Dave Berry, ABC star Martin Fry, actor Ian Reddington, boxing coach Brendan Ingle, Sheffield football legends Tony Currie and Derek Dooley, ice hockey star Ron Shudra and boxer Herol 'Bomber' Graham.

Before the dinner, more than 100 dignitaries attended the opening of the 'our150th' exhibition at the Millennium Galleries. The free event, which showcased Sheffield's unique history in the development of football and business, ran for a week and attracted more than 3,000 visitors.

Sheffield FC's new strip ahead of the 2007/08 season.

Chairman Richard Tims and manager Dave McCarthy at the re-enactment of the Sheffield Chamber of Commerce meeting.

Interest was so overwhelming that organisers had to extend it for an extra day to meet demand. Schools from across the area were also able to make a special trip to view the artefacts on show, with 350 pupils attending to learn about the city's history.

The exhibition featured a host of medals, trophies and caps from the city's prestigious football history, and prize exhibits included the original rules of the game, a winner's medal from Sheffield FC's 1904 Amateur Cup win and a replica of the 1966 World Cup presented to the club.

Other pieces included special memorabilia donated by Sheffield Wednesday, Sheffield United and the Sheffield & Hallamshire FA.

In May, Sheffield FC travelled to Asia to play in the invitational Philips Hong Kong Sevens football tournament, where they gave spirited performances against PSV Eindhoven and Tottenham Hotspur.

The event featured both young professional teams and legends from nine countries including France, Holland, South Africa, Japan, Australia, Singapore and Hong Kong. Matches involved seven players a side, playing two halves of seven minutes each at the Hong Kong Football Club stadium.

As part of the tournament, Sheffield FC also fielded a veterans' team. The side included former Sheffield Wednesday players Kevin Pressman and Danny Maddix, Sheffield United legends Bob Booker, Paul Wood, Tony Agana and Adrian Littlejohn plus ex-Chesterfield midfielder Chris Beaumont.

Sheffield FC manager Dave McCarthy and former Sheffield United player and current Club assistant manager Lee Walshaw were also in the squad.

Ahead of the tournament the club unveiled a new logo and image with a commemorative strip launched for the 2007/08 campaign after a kit deal

with international manufacturers Nike was agreed. The new look continued the club's commitment to developing a world-wide brand for the 21st century.

In the summer of 2007, Richard Tims proudly announced that FIFA president Sepp Blatter would be attending the club's 150th annual dinner on October 24 at the Cutlers' Hall.

Blatter has agreed to join the celebrations, along with Real Madrid president Ramon Calderon and it means that the dinner will rank among the biggest football events ever staged in the city with some of the most illustrious names in the game enjoying the anniversary.

Sheffield FC also announced pre-season games against Scottish giants Glasgow Rangers, Premiership side Blackburn Rovers, local rivals Sheffield Wednesday and Sheffield United and League One team Doncaster Rovers. The club will also play Hallam FC at Sandygate to re-enact the oldest fixture in world football.

Meanwhile, Sheffield FC ladies are set to face European Champions Arsenal ladies in a special fixture at the Bright Finance stadium. Last season Arsenal clinched every cup competition available in the women's game, winning 22 games out of 22.

Richard said: "We want to celebrate the birth of club football with the biggest figures in the game. For the president of FIFA and the president of Real Madrid to attend the dinner is a massive coup for the club and Sheffield.

"The support we have received from a number of top clubs has been unbelievable. It's great to continue the games between Sheffield and Glasgow as in those early days, with the friendly against Rangers. I'd like to thank everyone who has supported us during this special time for Sheffield FC.

"We want to use our anniversary year to show the world that the club is still active and continuing to give something back to the game 150 years on."

In connection with Real Madrid, Sheffield FC has helped produce a new photo book to mark the anniversary. Titled 'The Oldest and the Greatest,' the publication looks at the contrasts of the first club to the most successful, from the Bright Finance Stadium to the Estadio Santiago Bernabeu, and after that despite the differences between the two clubs, they both play the same game.

Chairman Richard Tims meets with Bobby Charlton at the joint 150th dinner.

Richard added: "The book shows one club at the highest pinnacle in world football and the other playing at grassroots level in England. Both are at completely different ends of the spectrum, but both playing exactly the same beautiful game."

Other activities the club are staging for the 150th year include a national disability tournament which will see the likes of Tottenham, Liverpool and Everton competing at the Bright Finance stadium and a children's football tournament, in association with McDonald's and Sheffield City Council, with local schools from the club's successful community scheme taking part.

The 150th anniversary has also led to Sheffield FC being invited to attend the qualifying draw for the 2010 South African World Cup in Durban in November 2007. As part of the connection with Africa, plans are in place for Club to play against the African Wanderers, one of the oldest clubs in South Africa after making a connection with the team during their Boots for Africa campaign.

150 Years of Memories

Alan Methley, current President of Sheffield FC.

"Having been associated with the club some 40 years I obviously have many happy memories. Sadly none are on the playing front as we did not win anything when I was playing!

"The biggest memory of course was sitting in the Royal Box at Wembley for the FA Vase Final. A close second, however, was representing the club at the FA's Centenary Cup Final Dinner in London – 1972.

"We were invited as a Founder Member of the FA. I was sat on a table of past winning captains next to Dave McKay (Spurs) and Frank McIntosh (Arsenal). It was a memorable experience.

"I also took the opportunity of trying to the sell the story of Club to Jimmy Hill and Danny Blanchflower (Spurs and Ireland captain) who in those days had a weekly column in the Sunday Express.

"The club was of no interest to Jimmy Hill, but Danny Blanchflower was interested and he spent five minutes or more with me listening about our history."

Steve Hall, secretary of Sheffield FC, who has been with the club for more than 20 years. Steve talks about the club's move to Owlerton Stadium.

"Mr Dave Allen and his A & S Leisure Group came to our rescue by allowing us to use Owlerton Greyhound Stadium. This would be the club's new home subject to the Northern Counties League ground grading report.

"The Sheffield United groundsman and his staff agreed to mark out the pitch before the inspection, but they called to say that the centre of the stadium was not big enough to get a full size pitch. They managed to get the full width but had to mark the length some five yards short of the required 110 yards! We decided to leave it as it was in the hope they wouldn't notice

"Frank Catt and Cliff Morris from the league carried out the inspection and found all the stadium facilities as very acceptable. However, the last part of their visit was to look at the playing surface and of course they found the problem.

"Much discussion took place and it was decided that because the pitch fell away to accommodate the speedway staged at the venue, the only solution would be to put portable corners in place before every match.

"As there was greyhound racing on a Friday night and each race was filmed, no work could be carried out until the day of the match. So for every game we had to bring the turf for the corner flags on special pallets to ensure they were laid level with the rest of the playing surface, line the new turf to make sure it matched the existing touch and goal lines and drill a hole to take the corner flags!

"Meanwhile, all the other committee members were deployed in carrying the goalposts, portable dug outs, goal nets and corner flags into position before the teams arrived.

"As there was racing again on Saturday night the goal posts and dug outs had to be returned to the storage points after the match. By the end of the day it was a toss up who was more tired, the players or the committee members! The 'joys' of providing facilities to keep your team playing four levels below the Football League."

Dave McCarthy, current team manager at Sheffield FC, on how he nearly quit the club.

"One autumn night in the 2006/07 season my Sheffield FC side were playing Maltby Main FC away.

"The game had been billed as a 'must-win' match for our club. In matches leading up to this game we had narrowly lost the Saturday previously in the FA Cup to Unibond Premier side Witton Albion, drawn the previous league game against Long Eaton and beaten Retford United FC on penalties in an early round of the FA Cup. Our form had been patchy and we were finding scoring goals an unexpected problem.

"Maltby Main can be a rather unforgiving place to be at any time of the year. The pitch was inconsistent, although well grassed and it was a chilly evening. It is also one of my former managerial clubs.

"I'd taken a gamble in leaving Chris Dolby, Jon Pickess and Chris White on the bench. Ryan O'Carroll came in for his first appearance of the season in centre midfield with ex-Maltby player Darren Winters unavailable.

"The game started well for Sheffield and it seemed it wouldn't be long before we would break the deadlock. As it transpired, Maltby took the lead midway through the half when a corner wasn't dealt with and the ball popped past a bewildered James Holmshaw in the Sheffield net.

"Club managed to go into the break 1-0 down and at half time I stressed that efforts were not good enough. We needed someone to take the game by the scruff of the neck, rise above any taunting received by the home supporters and show me how much it means to play for the oldest club in the world.

"The team seemed to be doing just that with Townsend and Powell going close before the hammer blow. Scott Somerville was brought down by Jones and a clear penalty was dispatched by the same player to make it 2-0 and spark off some unsavoury baiting. We were now vociferously branded as a waste of time and the Maltby faithful had already decided that no promotion was coming Sheffield FC's way that season.

"In the away dug out I wasn't sure at first whether I had the answer. I turned to the Sheffield FC goalkeeping coach Mark Joyce and away from earshot of anyone else blurted out 'sod it Joycey, I'm going four up-front and if it doesn't work that's me done'. Joycey laughed rather perplexed to hear such words from his manager.

"On 73 minutes, Jon Pickess, Chris White and Chris Dolby stripped off and replaced Gary Townsend, Gav Smith and Ryan O'Carroll. It was noticeable that the players coming off, rather than show any disgust at me for the decisions, looked embarrassed and a bit annoyed by all that was going on around them. The fella in the crowd shouted: "Bring 'em all off Macca, they're rubbish." At that point I glared and I don't know why, but I sensed that something special was about to happen.

"It was just three minutes later when the breakthrough came. A long throw across the area found Chris Dolby in a little space and he drove home superbly from 15 yards out. His celebration displaying, frustration, elation and determination and it told me much about the lad. Two minutes later a ball swung in from the left from Dolby saw Jon Pickess rise like a salmon at the back post and from a metre out he headed home to level the scores. As he was mobbed by his team mates we knew the script was written.

"It also appeared the gentleman behind me thought that too, as he couldn't get out of the stand quick enough and toddled off towards the exit before I could offer a wry smile that would answer his doubting comments.

A crowd picture from Hallam v Sheffield FC, October 1957. On the left of the image is George Follows, senior football writer for the *Daily Herald*, who died in the Munich Air Disaster just four months later. (*Daily Herald*)

"On 80 minutes, and before the supporter could reach the exit, the magical and possibly season changing moment arrived. Maltby struggled to clear the ball from their own area and the third sub, Chris White drove home a half volley that smashed into the back of the net and the comeback was complete. Club played out the remaining 10 minutes and kept the score at a remarkable 3-2 away win.

"Can you imagine how I felt having seen my lads never give up? To make a triple substitution, see all three players score within nine minutes of coming on to turn around a 2-0 deficit, is something I will always remember and I am sure many supporters will too.

"This was a game that could have been my last as the manager of Sheffield FC, but it turned out to be a game that kick started the whole season for us, giving the lads an inner strength that showed good sides are never beaten. We went unbeaten for eight games and set off on what turned out to be a wonderful and historic promotion campaign".

Dave Cartwright, Sheffield FC membership co-ordinator.

"I went with the club to the Hong Kong Football Club Masters' Sevens Tournament event in May 2007. The event was staged within the exotic and quite wonderful surroundings of the Happy Valley race course, on facilities most of us can only dream about.

"For everyone that made the trip it was the appearance of several of our current first team squad running out alongside the likes of Dutch giants PSV Eindhoven and Premiership side Tottenham Hotspur that set the nerves jangling.

"The boys performed heroically and were only narrowly defeated in the two games. In their final group game the team were trailing to local side Kitchee who had finished their domestic season as League runners up and Cup semi finalists. However, a creditable 1-1 draw meant the team finished third in their group.

"The magic moment had arrived when striker David Wilkins forced home a deserved equaliser for the Club. The rapturous support that followed from the crowd proved that Sheffield FC have become everyone's second favourite team."

Norman Cann, Mosborough, Sheffield

Norman played for Sheffield FC between 1955 – 1960 and was captain of the team during the Centenary year.

"The week before the anniversary we played against Hallam FC and lost 2-1. After the game someone asked: "Isn't the club 100 years old next week?" I replied that we were and had just played as if we were 100 years old!

"The person who asked the question turned out to be George Follows, a national sportswriter who died in the Munich disaster with the Manchester United side only a few months later.

"My brothers Ralf and Derek also played for the Club, but we were never in the same team. Ralf was a good centre-half and ended up signing professional terms with Mansfield Town.

"I joined Sheffield from Norton Woodseats as a forward, but when I arrived there was only the number two shirt available and I was asked to play at full-back for the time being. I ended up in that position for the whole of my time with the club and it worked out to be for the best.

"I have always said once a Sheffield Club player, always a Sheffield Club player. I will never forget the five years I had there, it was the best years of my life."

Raymond Mawhood, Old Whittington, Chesterfield

"My mother was the cook for Geoffrey Chambers, who was President of Sheffield FC at the time, and the son of the well-known former Club secretary Harry Waters Chambers. We lived with Geoffrey for a short while between 1949 to 1950 at his Victorian House on Westbourne Road in Sheffield.

"Geoffrey knew of my interest in football and showed me the medal his brother won playing for Sheffield Club in the 1904 Amateur Cup.

"When we were there, Geoffrey was renovating the house so he could take in lodgers, such as students, which is quite ironic now as those houses are now used for student accommodation.

"He was about 70 and I was 15 at the time. I found him a kind and genial person, who was always interested in my schooling and what I should do when I left school. He wanted me to take up carpentry, but my mother had other ideas and I ended up being a design draughtsman."

**Nigel Hughes
Former Sheffield FC player and now coach of the ladies team**

"I remember we played Queen's Park, the oldest

Geoffrey Chambers, Sheffield FC President until the early 1950s and the son of ex-Club secretary Harry Waters Chambers. (pic courtesy of Raymond Mawhood)

club in Scotland, on the hallowed turf at Hampden Park. When we arrived their club officials had put on a reception for us. They were very welcoming and offered us lots to eat and drink. It was a very merry evening!

"However, we kept asking when the Queen's Park players would arrive and each time they told us they were on their way. It didn't dawn on us until the next morning when we all woke up with huge hangovers that it was all a ploy. The Queen's Park players had never come out and were all fresh to play. Not surprisingly we were beaten in the match and we learnt a valuable lesson that day! We did get revenge when we played them the following year."

Richard Prest and his son George, descendants of William Prest.

"William was involved in an incident in a cricket match at Bramall Lane when Yorkshire were playing Surrey in 1861. The match had been abandoned due to a waterlogged pitch, but an angry crowd prevented the visiting side leaving the ground, the Surrey Captain William Caffyn being threatened by a gang of ruffians, the situation being made worse as the ground committee refused to pay the visitors' expenses.

"William, who at the time was Yorkshire Captain, declared that he was ashamed at the treatment of the visitors and, shaking with anger,

A team photo of Sheffield FC from the 1940s. (Pauline Reynolds image).

he followed the Surrey players onto the field and proceeded to hammer the runs required to complete a Yorkshire Victory!"

Pauline Reynolds from Sheffield.
Her father Frank Pashley played for Sheffield FC in the 1940s.

She added: "Dad began to play for Sheffield Club in 1942. He had been in the army, but came out after the Dunkirk evacuation as he was in a reserved occupation in the steelworks. He then went back in the army a couple of years later.

"His best friend was Bill Mullins who also played for Sheffield Club. Both played for Sheffield after the war and were part of the team which played in Eindhoven in 1947. They were even selected to play for the Sheffield and Hallamshire County FA side."

George Kent, Sheffield
A Sheffield FC supporter during the 1940s. George

has provided his memories of friend Frank Pashley. "Frank was a big centre forward and took some knocking off the ball. You don't see people like Frank anymore. He was never dirty and I was surprised after seeing him play for the Club why he wasn't taken up as a professional. He was certainly good enough."

Mrs. M. Webster, Chesterfield
Mrs. Webster's grandfather's uncle was Tommy Youdan, a theatre manager who put up trophies bearing his name for the first ever cup competition – the final of the Youdan cup took place at Bramall Lane, Sheffield on 5 March 1867. Hallam FC were the winners. Margaret's niece is Deidre Riseley who now works at the Coach and Horses pub next to the Sheffield FC ground.

"I remember that Tommy was good friends with Mr Bassett, who formed Bassett's Allsorts. When they died both left their savings to the house-keepers, who then left for America!

A team photo of Sheffield FC from around the early 1950s. (Pauline Reynolds image).

"At the time there wasn't much entertainment in Sheffield, so a lot of people went to Youdan's. We only found out there was a cup in his name last year, we didn't realise that it was probably one of the first in football."

John E. Mellows, Staveley

John, a centre-half, played against Sheffield FC during the 1951-52 season in a Yorkshire League game for South Kirkby Colliery. Club won 14-2 and the game took place at Abbeydale Park.

"Club had a centre forward called Geoff Robinson, a real will o' the wisp, speedy player. A name forever burned into my personal football past. Of the fourteen goals scored by Sheffield, Geoff scored nine!

"That night I did not buy the Sheffield *Green'Un* and perhaps centre half was not my best position! I received no criticism which is more than can be said of others in the defence. We lost to a far better team who coped with the conditions much more effectively than we did."

The result didn't affect John's playing career as he signed amateur forms with Blackpool FC, where he met football legend Sir Stanley Matthews.

Peter Beeby, Sheffield

Peter was chairman of Sheffield FC for five years before handing over the reigns to Richard Tims once the club had secured a new stadium in Dronfield.

"I became chairman around 1994-95 when the club was playing at Owlerton Stadium and in a worse state than the dogs! The Club was struggling to survive, especially with a large debt which made it difficult to build a team.

"We knew it was important to secure our own stadium, because the Club wouldn't progress if it was moving from pillar to post. There were a few of us who worked hard to see it through and eventually we agreed a deal to play home games on the Coach and Horses pitch.

"To then open the ground with a game against Manchester United and to have Richard Caborn there too was fantastic. It was a great reward for all the hard work everyone had put in."

Jon Ball, Sheffield FC's current matchday organiser.

"My sweetest moment arrived on 26 April when Club hosted Selby Town, our 11th game in 32 days. Selby had only to win their last two games to become League Champions. The night before we'd played a cup semi-final in Arnold and squeezed through after extra-time and penalties.

"Against Selby we had to put out a team more than half of whom were youngsters or non-regulars. Club went a goal down just after half time, but Mark Willgoose, injured for most of the season, broke clear down the left to equalise. He then set up Chris White for a late, late winner. All the team were heroes but only one was on the field for the whole of both games and indeed had scored the decisive penalty at Arnold in the cup. The usual five star from the Dronfield (Chris) Hilton.

"The funniest part was that I got chatting to a guy from the Goole Town Management who was stood near me that night. Goole could only take the Championship (and the sole promotion slot) if Selby slipped up.

"After we equalised I heard him on his mobile telling the people back in Goole that he was trying not to laugh. Heaven knows what he was doing after we won, I was too busy cheering and shouting to check! Goole won their last two games and, despite Selby winning their last fixture, Goole were Champions."

Craig Williamson, Sheffield FC's programme editor

"My greatest memory in the time I have been involved with Club so far must be the Senior Cup Final win at Hillsborough with a last minute winner against Worksop Town.

"The occasion was the first time in ten years that the club had reached this particular final and had a 'real' cup final atmosphere with it being played at Hillsborough.

"Worksop were hot favourites with them playing three divisions higher and had experience of games like this.

"Sheffield should have gone ahead early in the game when they missed a glorious chance. Throughout the game every man gave everything and we were the better side for the majority of the match.

"As the game looked destined for extra time the ball fell to Ben Cressey on the edge of the area who unleashed a superb strike which went in off the underside of the crossbar and start wild celebrations from everyone involved with the club.

"A magnificent performance and occasion for everyone connected with Sheffield FC."

Chris Stanley, Gainsborough

"I played for Club in 1965/1967 after being introduced to the team by Neil Warnock, who I knew from work. We played in one County Senior game at Manton Colliery and won 5-3 with Neil scoring all 5 and me saving 3 penalties.

"I returned as Coach in 1972 then brought in the late Roy Ford to manage the playing matters at the Club. Over a period we had John Warnock, Alan Stainrod and finally Dave Moxon looking after the Reserves.

"In 1972 the club had no second team and were languishing in the lower reaches of the Yorkshire League 3rd Division. The kit was so shrunk and washed out that the taller players had difficulty making the shorts and shirts meet. The stockings I leave to the imagination.

"Sometime during the period I was made Vice President. We took the Club to the 1st Division Yorkshire League, Yorkshire League Cup Winners and of course to the FA Vase Final in 1977."

Ray Taylor, Hope Valley, Sheffield

"I had the pleasure of playing for Sheffield Club in the year the Anglo-Dutch sports organisation was formed at the end of the Second World War. I scored against Eindhoven in our win there. My position in the side was outside right and Harry Parkin was our captain."

Happy Birthday Sheffield

IF ENGLAND is the motherland of football, then Sheffield FC are the midwife, having helped bring the sport kicking and screaming into the world 150 years ago. For people from Rio to Reykjavik, the thought of a world without football would be unbearable. So, thank you, Sheffield for setting the ball rolling 150 years ago. You gave life to the club game.

The fact that the president of FIFA, Sepp Blatter, has taken such an interest in the club speaks volumes for Sheffield FC's place in football's history. Real Madrid's friendship with Sheffield FC highlights the respect everyone in football feels for 'the world's oldest club'. You will have some impressive friends to help you blow out the 150 candles.

Sheffield FC are older than Manchester United, Chelsea, Celtic, and even mighty Madrid themselves. Those few words 'The World's Oldest Club' mean so much. Every club are in Sheffield FC's debt for setting a trend, shaping a sport, even coming up with the Sheffield Rules and promoting the introduction of free-kicks and corners. Many current clubs could learn from Sheffield FC's founding principles of integrity, respect and community.

But Sheffield FC are not simply about the past. The future promises much. Timing is an essential quality in sport so it is particularly pleasing to see Sheffield FC currently on the rise, celebrating their 150 years with a place in Northern Premier League Division One.

The presence of 13 junior sides indicate a club looking to the future. Here's to the next 150 years. Happy Birthday.

Henry Winter
Football Correspondent
Daily Telegraph.
September 2007

Acknowledgements

THE IDEA to develop a book on Sheffield FC's history would never have got off the ground had it not been for the vision of the club Chairman, Richard Tims. He has encouraged every stage and has been an enthusiastic supporter throughout the whole process.

Richard has worked tirelessly to establish the club's unique position in world football and deserves great credit for the job he has done.

This book should be seen as an attempt at a serious history of Sheffield Football Club. There is no suggestion that it is a thoroughly referenced academic work. Certainly no detailed endnotes have been included as it was felt that the text needed to be readable rather than overly complex. A lengthy bibliography has been inserted and it is hoped that this will suffice for future researchers and students of the history of the game.

A history of Sheffield FC by Fred Walters, published in 1957 to coincide with the centenary, already exists. However, there would have been little point in simply regurgitating the information of the previous book. As a result, the text in this book moves the story on in several areas:

More information is provided on the co-founders of the club, Nathaniel Creswick and William Prest.

The first playing rules, which are incorrectly transcribed in the 1957 edition, have been amended.

The encounters between the London and Sheffield Associations have been put under further scrutiny. In fact for the initial encounter, the Sheffield team was not a representative eleven, but rather one from Sheffield FC itself.

Sheffield's footballers have been highly influential on the development of the modern game. The innovations of the members of the local association have shaped the sport through the introduction of many original laws.

The stories behind Sheffield's early FA Cup exploits, together with the Amateur Cup triumph of 1904, have also been dealt with in more detail.

Finally, the club's list of international players has been updated.

The most important place for any research into the history of a football club is undoubtedly the local library. The staff at the Local Studies section of Sheffield Central Library have always been helpful and obliging. Similar sentiments can be expressed about their colleagues down the road at Sheffield Archives.

A big thank you must also go to Sheffield Newspapers and Alan Powell, editor of *Sheffield Star* and *Green'Un*, particularly, to allow us to use information, pictures and clippings.

Vital to the early days of the club was William Prest. It required a good deal of research through Cambridge University records to trace one of William's brothers, Edward, who attended St John's College. This information was vital to the understanding of the type of football played in Sheffield and was provided by a good friend, John Smith, at Trinity College, Cambridge.

Professor Eric Dunning at Leicester University has read a draft of this book and suggested a few amendments. He remains an inspiration.

As always, David Barber at the Football Association has given his time and advice with equal measure and can always be relied upon to provide quality information. Thanks also go to Adrian Harvey, whose research on Sheffield football has been quite intensive and who kindly agreed to the use of his table on the occupations of the early football pioneers.

Telephone conversations with John Steele, the author of the history of Hallam FC, Sheffield's rivals, have been thought-provoking and extremely stimulating.

May we also thank all those tens of people who have supplied pictures, information, anecdotes and newspaper clippings of Sheffield FC's history. There are too many to mention all here, however, the book would not be what it is without your support.

This acknowledgement also includes anyone else whose work, either photographic or editorial, has been used or referred to in the preparation of this book.

Finally, Graham Curry's wife Judy deserves much credit in putting up with his endless visits to Sheffield Library. She has been understanding and even engaged Graham in conversation over his findings!

Select Bibliography

Allaway, R. 2001. *Soccer in the United States, 1900-1920.*

Booth, J. T. 1976. *The Development of Sheffield Amateur Sports Club 1911 to 1956.*

Brown, T. 1996. *The Official History of Notts. County: 1862-1995.* Harefield: Yore Publications. pp.14-15.

FA News. 1957. *The Official Journal of the Football Association.*

Farnsworth, K. 1995. *Sheffield Football: A History Volume I 1857-1961.* Sheffield: The Hallamshire Press.

Farnsworth, K. 1995. *Sheffield Football: A History Volume II 1961-1995.* Sheffield The Hallamshire Press.

Goodman, P. and Hutton, S. 2005. *150 Years of Bramall Lane. Sheffield United FC.* Sheffield: Northend Limited.

Goulstone, J. 2001. *Football's Secret History: A 3-2 Sporting Retrospective.* Upminster: 3-2 Books.

Green, G. 1953. *A History of the Football Association.* London: Naldrett Press.

Harris, N. 2003. 'England, Their England: The Definitive Story of Foreign Footballers in the English Game Since 1888.* Pitch Publishing.

Harvey, A. 2001. 'An Epoch in the Annals of National Sport: Football in Sheffield and the Creation of Modern Soccer and Rugby'. *International Journal of the History of Sport.* (December).

Harvey, A. 2005. *Football: The First Hundred Years. The Untold Story.* Abingdon: Routledge.

Lamming, D. 1987. *A Scottish Soccer Internationalists' Who's Who: 1872-1986.* Beverley: Hutton Press. p.117.

Marples, M. 1954. *A History of Football.* London: Secker & Warburg.

Shearman, M. 1888. *Athletics and Football.* London: Longmans, Green & Co.

Sparling, R.A. 1926. *The Romance of the Wednesday.* Sheffield: W.C. Leng & Co Ltd.

Vickers, J.E. 1978. *A Popular History of Sheffield.* Sheffield: Applebaum Bookshop Ltd.

Walters, F. 1957. *Sheffield Football Club Centenary History.* Sheffield: Allen & Unwin.

Young, P. 1962. *Football in Sheffield.* London: Stanley Paul and Co. Ltd.

Young, P. 1968. *A History of British Football.* London: Sportsman's Book Club.

Newspaper Archival Sources
Daily Herald newspaper
Sheffield Newspapers Ltd.
Sheffield City Library
Sheffield Archives
Sheffield and Rotherham Independent, 21 February 1876 and 3 April 1876.